D0870191

called
to
service

by
Joseph Lange, OSFS
and
Anthony J. Cushing

**VOLUME IV
OF THE
LIVING CHRISTIANITY COMMUNITY
SERIES**

DOVE PUBLICATIONS
Pecos, New Mexico

PAULIST PRESS
New York, N.Y./Paramus, N.J.

Acknowledgements

Scripture quotations, unless otherwise noted, were taken from *The New American Bible*, with the permission of the Confraternity of Christian Doctrine.

Quotations marked JB are taken from *The Jerusalem Bible*, Doubleday and Company, Garden City, N.Y., copyrighted by Darton, Longman and Todd, Ltd., and Doubleday and Co., Inc., 1966.

Quotations marked TEV are taken from *Good News for Modern Man: The New Testament in Today's English Version*, copyrighted by the American Bible Society, 1966.

NIHIL OBSTAT
Msgr. James Mulligan
Censor Librorum

IMPRIMATUR
Most Rev. Joseph McShea, D.D.
Bishop of Allentown
December 4, 1975

Copyright ©1976 by
Paulist Fathers, Inc.
and Dove Publications

Library of Congress
Catalog Card Number: 75-41813

Published by
Paulist Press
Editorial Office: 1865 Broadway, N.Y., N.Y. 10023
Business Office: 400 Sette Drive, Paramus, N.J. 07652

ISBN 0-8091-1921-8

and
Dove Publications
Benedictine Abbey
Pecos, N.M. 87552

Printed and bound in the
United States of America

Table of Contents

Introduction

This is the fourth (and final) volume in a series of instructions about the Christian vision and Christian life. More than with the other three volumes we are aware of the incompleteness of what is presented in the following chapters. We see very clearly that what we have written serves only as an introduction, but that is consistent with what we have set out to do. We have not attempted to re-write the Gospels, but only to offer some insights on how to interpret them.

Jesus offers us a total vision of life and the power of His Spirit to live it. He selected twelve men to be with Him as He presented different parts to different audiences so that at least these twelve would have the whole vision. He shared His Spirit with them that they might recall all of it. That vision is contained in the Gospels.

Let us make no mistake about it, the vision of Jesus is revolutionary. It touches every aspect of our lives, from understanding ourselves to understanding the world to understanding how to relate to each other. His teaching is a judgment on every aspect of life, on every detail of it. To be a follower of Jesus is to put on His mind, to enter into that vision and to live it out.

In our first volume, *Friendship with Jesus*, we were primarily concerned with the initial steps of encountering Jesus, entering into a personal relationship with Him and receiving His Spirit. In these succeeding volumes we have attempted to elaborate the vision as it applies to our life together.

There are lots of distortions about what it really means to follow Jesus, and these abound in every denomination and in every sect. By and large we have not concerned ourselves with arguing with other interpretations. We have seen our task as presenting, proclaiming the Gospel in the light of the best scholarship we could find. The search for truth has been a hard and long one. Ill-prepared and false teachers abound, so the responsibility we felt in preparing these teachings has not been taken lightly.

Mindful that Jesus calls us to abundant life, to power in the Spirit, to receiving and giving forgiveness, to receiving and giving love, to freedom, to joy and peace, to personal responsibility and to a life together, we know that all of these things must be preserved and balanced without compromise and with total commitment. It is to this formidable task that we have given ourselves in the Children of Joy community in Allentown, Pa. It is our experience that we share with you.

We make mistakes, lots of mistakes. We sometimes have felt that we have been wandering around the desert like the Jews with Moses. At other times we have felt that we have been on Tabor. The point is, not that we are perfect, but that we *know* that the Gospel can be lived without compromise, that we can grow together into a people of God, that He can and does gradually transform us, that He is real and His love for us is real.

Most of all, we know that Jesus is the Way, the Truth, and the Life.

May the Lord bless you in all of your life, in all that you do, in all that you are. May He be praised forever.

Joseph Lange, OSFS
Anthony Cushing

by Anthony Cushing

Gifts for Service ▯

(The Ministries of the Body of Christ)

The easiest way for me to talk about gifts and ministries is to describe our experience in the Children of Joy community. Not only does this keep things practical but it conveys a sense of growth and process. And we did grow in our understanding and use of the gifts of the Spirit. This growth came through mistakes as often as successes, which is the way it usually happens with human beings. After appreciation of the lived witness, then it will be easier to tackle the more theoretical understanding of the gifts.

Our community didn't start as a charismatic group. We began through a series of retreats for young adults, and from that we met together weekly for prayer and sharing. Our style of prayer was basically conversational prayer as described by Rosalind Rinker. There was a lot of enthusiasm and spontaneous love in the group. People were encountering Jesus in a very meaningful, although emotional, way. This led to a very powerful and joyful witnessing and in less than three months there were over 100 people at our prayer meetings.

The power of the Spirit worked in us even though we weren't too aware of who the Spirit was or what He did. We simply trusted in Jesus and He heard us. Through prayer we discovered that we had just the right words when witnessing to someone. There were all kinds of *coincidences* such as meeting the right people at the right time which spoke of some kind of guidance by Jesus. There were even a few healings. The most amazing was a 3 year-old child who had spinal meningitis and who had never spoken or stood up in her life. The day after we prayed she stood up and started talking, and the doctors could find no trace of the spinal meningitis. So, people learned and were thankful for the power of God.

We were anonymous charismatics who only needed to understand and consciously expect the power of the Spirit. The only gifts that weren't manifested were prophecy and tongues. There was the same experience in the Cursillo movement in the area, with whom we were closely connected.

There were also glaring weaknesses. The group seemed too dependent on human affection and group dynamics. There was a sense of faddishness, that this was a once-a-week spiritual fix. And conversational prayer with a hundred people became rapidly boring. It was obvious that we needed something.

About that time our spiritual director recommended that we try out a charismatic workshop. We did, and of the 150 people attending, *10 people* asked to be baptized in the Spirit. These ten realized the need to grow in this new awareness of the Spirit, so we started meeting apart from the conversational group. Here we learned how to be open to the gifts of the Spirit that Paul talks about in I Corinthians 12. We also discovered that when we prayed with people to be baptized in the Spirit, the same things happened to them that happened to us. Almost everyone who desired the gift of tongues received it.

About this time people other than our pastor got involved in service. Because we needed to explain about the Charismatic Renewal, people were asked to teach and be discussion leaders in retreats and classes. This was all rather informal; a teacher would ask some people to help him in the classes and that was it. A little later we also felt the need to be in touch with people, so we formed small prayer groups, and the leaders of those groups got together to simply talk about how things were going. Later on we saw this to be the beginnings of the pastoral and teaching ministries.

Other services developed out of the needs of the community. Someone had to respond to the very basic physical needs that any group of people has. Chairs had to be set up for our prayer meetings, a rudimentary bookstore had to be maintained, and some kind of secretarial agility was needed just to keep up with all of the people who were coming and going.

After we had been meeting together for about 8 months, there was a dramatic change in our prayer group. Most of the people attending were young adults and students who had experienced God through a retreat program. By this time about 70 of us had been prayed with for the release of the Spirit. Well, what happened was that an older prayer group from another city felt God leading them to join with us, so one night about 100 people came into our core group. What made it even more interesting was that they were mostly older married couples and clergy. They wondered why we were so exuberant; we wondered why they were so quiet. "Why do you breathe so heavily when you prophesy?" they asked. Our answer was, "Why do you say 'Hail Mary' every time someone says the Our Father?" We went barefoot and sat on the floor; they got dressed up and liked to "socialize" after the prayer meeting. In short, we experienced all the normal difficulties that come up when people from different lifestyles try to get together. To top it all off, our leader was away for most of the next three months, leaving a few young and inexperienced people to try to take care of things. That group found out that good intentions weren't enough to deal with the complexities of building community. The result was a kind of baptism of suffering in which we lost about half the people in the group. But we learned a lot about service and how to love each other. The older people brought a sense of stability and a lot of common sense to the younger people's enthusiasm. We learned a lot of little things like:

- trying to be punctual;
- study and hard work are real gifts to the community;
- mundane jobs were often the test of our commitment;
- sensitivity to people's needs was the basic way to express love.

With all of this our sense of community grew as we learned both to accept each other in weakness and to challenge each other to responsibility. After we expressed our commitment in a covenant we found out that we really didn't know what that meant until we tried and failed over and over to live up to that commitment. We saw very clearly that to experience trust in each other we needed to experience each other's trustworthiness. This was especially difficult for me, and I was especially difficult for the community. Rather frequently I would attempt some kind of service and then fail to come through with it. But the group continued to encourage me until finally an overdue fruit called faithfulness started to appear. This was how it went with many people. We had a sense of experimentation about discovering our particular gift. Some people tried out teaching only to find out that they felt much more comfortable just offering hospitality and friendship to newcomers. A few flung themselves into every available opportunity for service and most often found themselves burned out after a few months. Others simply waited for God to open up something for them.

Gradually as our commitment to God grew, our outreach started to grow also. At first almost all the service in the community was directed to the prayer meetings. However, more and more, our Christian life became something shared outside of prayer meetings. People became more active in their parishes. At the same time we were frequently asked to send teams to other cities to share what God had done for us. We needed people to do typing and printing. Some people felt drawn to running a children's program. Another group started running a coffeehouse where people could have a low profile encounter with a Christian community. Then there were the J.C. Movers which specialized in no-cost moving for our very mobile apartment dwellers. We were given a 32-acre farm and someone had to take care of that. We also plodded through a total renovation of our Center which took an excruciating nine months. All of this took time and money and people were called to share more and more of both.

Interestingly enough one of the responses to all of this activity was that we found out that we needed to learn how to relax and have fun together. A few people really enjoyed giving parties and picnics, and the Spirit used this talent to teach all of us how to play as well as pray together. This led into a very beautiful way of celebrating the marriages that took place in our community. Practically everyone in the community would contribute time and food to give each couple a joyful wedding and reception. The result is that through the parties, coffeehouses, and weddings a whole group of people who would never go to a prayer meeting have been touched by the love and joy of a Christian community.

I am describing our community not to set up a model of how communities should develop, but to give a sense of the process of growing into service. I am *de*scribing what happened, I am *not* *pre*scribing what should happen in other groups.

Reflecting on this kind of experience we see that the Spirit works through the ordinary facts of our lives. There are the spectacular witnesses of physical and psychological healings coming from our healing teams. There are dramatic conversions and breakthroughs through the teaching ministry. But the life in the Spirit is a *life*, and life has its drama but is more often concerned with the little miracles among family and friends. The charismatic gifts of service have become more ordinary because that's where most of our life is. More and more we need to expect the Spirit to break into our everyday life: to make our homes centers of tenderness and hospitality. We realize the need to develop our creativity and our hunger for beauty, to make even our phone conversations occasions of God's healing. What we see then is the Spirit using our talents and love, the failures and miracles, to create a whole new way of life. At first it seems very ordinary, just as the separate pieces of a mosaic are ordinary. The Spirit joins them together to create a miracle of beauty.

> And that we might live no longer for ourselves but for him (Jesus), he sent the Holy Spirit from you, Father, as his first gift to those who believe, to complete his work on earth and bring us the fullness of grace. (Eucharistic Prayer IV— Roman Liturgy)

This is both a prayer and a statement of fact. All Christians are to carry on the work of Jesus through the power of the Holy Spirit. This seems to be a bit presumptuous. After all, we are just humans, ordinary people. And Jesus? Well, Jesus was Jesus, right? Maybe this applies just to the saints or to priests and ministers? And Jesus says:

> I tell you most solemnly, whosoever believes in me will perform the same works as I do myself, he will perform even greater works, because I am going to the Father (John 14:12-13).

5

I've quoted this passage to many people while on retreats and the most frequent response is, "Did he really say that?" I can understand this skepticism because, for most of us, this isn't a matter of our daily experience. Most people feel a need to rationalize this away because they rightly feel "If this is true, then I must be missing something." What does it mean then to carry on the work of Jesus? How does it happen in my life? Before I get into this, we have to take a brief look at the ministry of Jesus. The idea here is not to give a detailed account but an overall impression of the mission of Jesus.

THE MESSIANIC PRESENCE

Jesus came to love, and became man out of love for us. Everything He did is best understood as an expression of His saving love for us. Love is the context of the ministry of Jesus. Love is the motivation and the end of all that Jesus has in store for us. This is why His commandment is for us to "love one another as I have loved you" and, as St. John writes: "Anyone who lives in love lives in God, and God lives in him" (John 4:10). So Jesus' ministry is the work of love. To illustrate that this is also *our* work of love, I want to parallel some scriptural passages which describe Jesus' ministry and what He asks us to do.

He proclaimed the Good News from God (Mark 1:15) and revealed the Father, "when you see me you see the Father" (John 14). In the same way Jesus says to us: Go out to the whole world; proclaim the Good News to all creation (Mark 16:16).

Jesus healed and worked wonders: When asked by John's disciples for proof that he was the Messiah, Jesus said, "Go back and tell John what you have seen and heard: the blind see again, the lame walk, lepers are cleansed, and the deaf hear; the dead are raised to life, the Good News is proclaimed to the poor and happy is the man who does not lose faith in me" (Luke 7:22-23).

He says that we will "do the same works that I do" and one

of the signs associated with believers is that "they will lay their hands on the sick who will recover" (Mark 16:18).

Jesus expresses who he is by dying for us in love: "I am the good shepherd . . . for these sheep I will give my life" (John 10). "If a man loses his life for my sake, he will save it."

Jesus is anointed with the Spirit and is the one who baptizes in the Holy Spirit and we are to be "filled with the Holy Spirit."

Jesus forgives in love and we are to "forgive one another as God has forgiven you."

"As the Father sent me so too I send you. Whoever receives you receives me" (John 20:21).

As Yves Congar pointed out, the verb "to send" in Aramaic (*saliah*) implies the total representation of an ambassador who has the same power and authority as the one he represents. As St. Augustine once said: "Let us rejoice with great thanksgiving for we are not only Christians but Christs." All of this is summed up in an Eastern Orthodox saying: "He became like us so that we might become like Him."

This is why Vatican II re-emphasized the active ministry of the laity as participating in the ministry of Jesus.

They are in their own way made sharers in the priestly, pro-phetic and kingly functions of Christ. They carry out their own part in the mission of the whole Christian people with respect to the Church and the world.[1]

So, when St. Paul proclaims that "You, then, are the Body of Christ" (1 Corinthians 12:14), he is not just speaking meta-phorically. The Christian community is the presence of Jesus in

[1] *The Documents of Vatican II*, ed. Walter B. Abbott, S.J. (New York: The America Press, 1966), p. 57. All quotations from Vatican II in this book are taken from this source.

the world. To encounter the body of believers is to encounter in the same way the risen Jesus. To encounter the community is to encounter the love and forgiveness of Jesus, to experience the power of Jesus in the Spirit through healing and deliverance. It is to encounter the Good News lived in the love of everyday persons and preaching "a crucified Christ . . . who is the power and the wisdom of God" (1 Corinthians 2:5). The church-community then is the messianic presence and in it one experiences the love and power of Jesus who is "with us all days, even to the end of the world."[2]

Now, if the community is the messianic presence, each person in the community is an active part of that body which serves as Jesus did.

No part of the structure of a living body is merely passive but *each has a share in the function as well as in the life of the body.* . . . Indeed so intimately are the parts linked and interrelated in this body (cf. Eph. 4:16) that the member who fails to make his proper contribution to the development of the Church must be said to be useful neither to the Church nor to himself (*Decree on the Apostolate of the Laity*, p. 491).

So every person in the community is to play a part in being the loving presence of Jesus. Since many of us do not experience this as an everyday reality in our church-communities a good question is, "Why doesn't this happen?" To answer this you have to talk about why it does happen.

Paul says that "each of you has been given some manifestation of the spirit (or service gift) for the common good" (R.S.V. 1 Cor. 12:7). This comes about because "we were all baptized in the one Spirit" and all the gifts "are the work of the one and the same Spirit, who distributes different gifts to different people just as he chooses." (1 Cor. 12:11). So anyone who is open to the Holy Spirit can exercise this loving service of the Body of Christ. Of course, the question is now "who is open to the Holy Spirit?"

[2]There is not a total identification of the Body of Christ and the risen Christ. The Church is not a new Incarnation. She is also the Bride of Christ being purified of her sinfulness in preparation for the eschatological marriage to Jesus. (Rev. 21)

The Sacrament of Baptism is "being begotten of water and Spirit" (Jn. 3:5). If the baptized Christian continues in a loving relationship with Jesus, then the Holy Spirit lives in him. Those who break off or never have a loving relationship with Jesus, renounce the gift of the Spirit given to them in Baptism. We, as adults, have to say "yes" to what God did for us in the Sacrament of Baptism. This is the same as when we personally accept or appropriate *now* what Jesus did for us in His life, death, and resurrection. This makes the historical reality of being saved a personal and present experience. Now many of us have renewed our relationship with Jesus and have been "baptized in the Holy Spirit." We personally renewed and experienced what happened to us in Baptism and experienced the gifts of the Holy Spirit. This is not limited to Pentecostals for "the Spirit blows where he will" (John 3). *Any baptized Christian is open to the power of the Holy Spirit through his relationship with Jesus.*

This makes sense because God will give us the power to do what He asks of us. If Jesus commands all Christians to love as He loves then He's going to give us the power to do so. If Jesus promises that we "will do the works" that He does and heal as He does, then He will give all of us the power to do so. This means that the loving power of the Spirit is *available* to all Christians. If this is true, then why don't more baptized Christians avail themselves of this power for loving service? Of course, there are those who neither want nor have a loving relationship with Jesus. Aside from this I would say that most Christians *do not understand* their everyday lives in terms of the power of the Spirit. Because of this they do not have the *faith to expect* the Spirit to work in them in this way.

Some do not understand that this Christian life is a challenge to loving service. Others believe this but have no concept or experience of how the Holy Spirit is to inspire this service. Some think that all of this is the job of the priests. Others have no community involvement which is the arena of the service gifts. Most of this is the result of inadequate teaching and the lack of community witness of faith and service.

So then what we need to do is:

1. Understand *what* these gifts are.

2. Realize *how* they operate.
3. *Choose* to use them out of love.
4. Yield to the power of the Spirit.

WHAT ARE THE GIFTS OF SERVICE?

If we look at Jesus, we see that in addition to His ministry He was a "man like us in all things but sin." That means that Jesus lived a normal human life as the God-man. He didn't do some things as God and other things as man. Everything he did from everyday carpentry work, to His miracles and dying on the cross, He did as Jesus the God-man. You could say then, that everything He did, He did "full of the Spirit."

In this way, Jesus sanctified every aspect of human life. There is no longer any separation between the natural and the supernatural because they are joined in Jesus.

This is important to keep in mind because some people misunderstand the words "spiritual" or "supernatural" to be anti-material or anti-human. By this reasoning, the less human and the less material a gift is, the more "spiritual" it is.

To these people, the gift of tongues is therefore more spiritual than visiting the sick. Now it is true that the scriptural writers contrast "spiritual" and "living in the Spirit" with "natural" and "living in the Flesh." However, the "natural man" is self-centered, isolated and hostile to God. It has nothing to do with your body or materiality as such. A "spiritual man" is God-centered and loving. Because of Jesus' Incarnation, there is no longer any separation between the natural and the supernatural. As one theologian says, Jesus shows us "a divine way of being human and a human way of being divine."

Understanding this, we can see that our whole lives can be lived in the power of the Spirit. It's not just at prayer meetings or in miracles that spiritual gifts can operate. Every aspect of our everyday lives, from housework to politics, can be a work of the Spirit.

There is a beautiful synthesis of the natural and supernatural in the Offertory prayers of the Mass which was also the Hebrew grace:

Blessed are you, Lord, God of all creation. Through your

goodness we have this bread to offer, which earth has given and human hands have made. It will become for us the bread of life.

Notice that there are three elements to what will be the Body of Christ:
1. the gift of God,
2. what nature has given,
3. work of man.

In the same way our service to the Church is always a gift of God's Spirit expressed in and through what nature has given and man has made. In this way all creation and man's work are united and made holy by the Spirit.

We can have problems with this if we continue to think of spiritual gifts as "things we receive." In this, like the old analogy of sanctifying grace *filling* a milk bottle, you get a part of a prophecy or a quantity of healing. This is partially the fault of using language like "getting a gift" or receiving "*the* Baptism in the Holy Spirit." This misses the whole point of "spiritual gifts and activity" as a *relationship* with the Holy Spirit. In this sense of relationship, Killian McDonald says "*that the gifts are not so much a what but a how.*" A spiritual gift is a way of doing something (practically anything) in the Spirit. The gift of tongues is a way of praising in the power of the Holy Spirit. The gift of knowledge is a way of teaching in the power of the Spirit. To look at the gifts this way is not to deny their basic character as a gift from God. Not all teaching or praying is a service gift. You can teach and pray without the power of the Spirit. What God gives is His presence plus the power of the Holy Spirit, and this we can never earn or deserve.

This comes out more clearly with the gift of tongues. Not all praying in tongues is a spiritual gift. There is a remote possibility that it might be inspired by the devil. There is also the greater possibility that once God gives someone the ability to pray in tongues they use it for their own interests. If a person gets up at a parish Mass and starts speaking in tongues just to show off his spiritual superiority then I don't think you could call this a gift inspired by the Holy Spirit. Also, sometimes people just make an honest mistake about an inspiration. In other words, praying in tongues can be a gift that builds up the community one week and the next week it won't be this kind of gift but merely the activity of praying in tongues without the Spirit. This is just a matter of our experience. So then, just because somebody performs the *activity of* prophecy, witnessing, or even marriage or celibacy, this doesn't necessarily mean it's a gift of the Holy Spirit. How many people get married without ever thinking of or wanting the power of the Spirit to make that marriage a gift. So it's not so much what you do as the way you do it (in the Spirit) that matters. I'll add some qualifications to this later on.

If we look at the *way* Jesus did things, we can see some basic ingredients for giving service in the power of the Spirit. Jesus did things out of love for the sake of others. He did this as the Father directed Him and for the glory of the Father (John 12:49). We, too, are to exercise the gifts God gives to us in love for others to the glory of the Father. This can be something extraordinary or something very routine. If we look at Jesus' first miracle at Cana, we see both these aspects. Jesus performs an amazing sign of changing the water into wine. This is done to meet a very ordinary human need and to bring people joy. Some Scripture scholars see this as symbolic of Jesus' gift of the Spirit in the new covenant. The Jewish religion "has no wine"; it does not have the joy and vitality of life that only the wine of the Spirit can bring. So, Jesus gives the people wine so that they can celebrate. He gives them a lot of wine, something like 120 gallons of the best. Now, if something as down to earth as supplying wine for a party is a miracle symbolizing the gift of the Spirit, then it is clear to me that almost anything we do through the power and guidance of God is a spiritual gift. This is St. Paul's principle in describing a charismatic life:

> *Whatever you do in word or work*, do all in the name of the Lord Jesus Christ, giving thanks to God the Father through Him (Colossians 3:17).

DIVERSITIES OF GIFTS

When Paul gives us lists of the charisms it doesn't seem that he is saying that these are the only charisms there are. There are differences in each list. For example:

I Corinthians 12	*Romans 12*	*1 Corinthians 12:28*
wisdom	prophecy	apostles
knowledge	service	prophets
faith	teaching	teachers
healing	encouragement	wonder-workers
miracles	distribution (finances)	healers
prophecy	authority	helpers
discernment	almsgiving	administrators
tongues		tongue speakers
interpretation		

1 Corinthians 7:7	*Ephesians 4:11*	*1 Corinthians 13:1-3*
marriage	apostles	tongues
celibacy	prophets	prophecy
	evangelists	knowledge
	teachers	faith
		poverty through almsgiving
		martyrdom

First of all, Paul sometimes refers to gifts that any Christian is open to: "I would like all of you to speak in tongues; but I would rather that all of you prophesy" (1 Corinthians 14:5). At other times he seems to be talking about a kind of public office or ministry which is a bit more regular and specialized:

All of you then are Christ's body, and each one is a part of it. In the church then, God has put all in place: in the first place Apostles, in the second place, prophets, and in the third place teachers. . . . They are not all Apostles, or prophets or teachers (1 Corinthians 12:27-29).

This means that while everyone can prophesy not everyone is a prophet. This is just to say that each person has his part and ministry in the body that he regularly performs. This is not all that they do, however. The teacher is still open to the gifts of prophecy, tongues, etc., and has a responsibility to use that gift when the Spirit inspires him. This is much different from our

13

prevalent attitude toward the priesthood and the ministry. Many lay people feel that since it is the job of the priests to preach the Gospel they should never evangelize someone. Parents think that only nuns and teachers should communicate the faith to their children and then get angry because their children don't exhibit the values that they failed to teach them. This is not entirely the fault of the laity, for often they have been made to feel inadequate to any task except giving money. When only professionals can evangelize, visit the sick, or give wise counsel, then one must surmise that perhaps the Spirit is no longer a free gift to all but a just reward for those with adequate training.

Laying the burden of service on priests, religious, and the ministry is not only bad for the laity but for the ministers as well. People expect from them services for which God might not have given them the talent or grace to perform. Men who are excellent pastors and teachers are expected to be financial geniuses as well. Gifted counselors and artists end up teaching grade school religion. Thank God that Vatican Council II has opened the door to a broader concept of ministry which calls all Christians to serve in the Church. This restores a more biblical approach to authority as service of leadership where the pastors

> understand that it is their noble duty so to shepherd the faithful and recognize their services and charismatic gifts that all, according to their proper roles, may cooperate in the common understanding with one heart (*Constitution on the Church*, p. 57).

This wisdom, along with the charismatic experience that all believers can be open to the gifts of the Spirit, will once again make our churches places where everyone can say, "To each person the manifestation of the Spirit is given for the common good" (1 Corinthians 12:8).

CHARISMS IN THE 20TH CENTURY

The Spirit works in each person according to the talents and limitations of that person. This is just to say that the Spirit works in real people in real historical situations. For example, Sts. Paul and John had beautiful gifts of literary expression that St. Mark didn't have. Not only that, but all of them had the limitations of their particular cultures. They couldn't readily imagine a culture without slavery or male dominance.

In the charismatic experience it is easy for us to identify with the apostolic experience of the Spirit. We, too, speak in tongues, prophesy, and witness healings and miracles. However, there are important differences in our real situation, which means that the Spirit will be working in new and different ways. *There are different charisms for different situations.* Television, radio, psychology, medicine, politics, music, art, economics, etc., all are ways in which the Spirit can be active in modern Christians. That these charisms are not mentioned in Scripture is no more surprising than Genesis not being a scientific treatise. We do not have to try to fit these modern charisms into a scriptural box by calling a television ministry the gift of knowledge, for example. We must be wary of making our prayer groups what one theologian calls "a first century Bible fantasy land." We do not have to have the same structure and use the same labels that Paul did. We are a different people and culture, and the Spirit moves in us as we are now with the glories and horrors of our own age.

Before we go on, I want to summarize what I've said so far:

1. We are called to be the Body of Christ to "complete His work on earth."
2. The Spirit gives us the power to live as Jesus lived.
3. Every aspect of our life is open to the power of the Spirit.
4. Charisms (gifts) of the Spirit are not things, but ways of giving service, open to all believers.
5. The Spirit works through, and in spite of, our personal and cultural realities.

EXPECTANT FAITH

One night at one of our prayer meetings a dear and beautiful nun, Sr. Jean, told a little story: She had been praying for faith and asked the Lord to give her the "faith of Abraham." As she continued to pray she felt the Lord say to her, "I don't want you to have the faith of Abraham, I want you to have the faith of Jean." God will give us the faith and power to meet the needs and opportunities of our day-to-day life.

I think this is extremely important to remember. Many of us hear or read witnesses of the great things God does in other people's lives and then feel guilty because we are not great healers or evangelists. We create images of what a real Christian should be and try to force ourselves into the mold. I don't have to be a St. Francis or John Wesley or Kathryn Kuhlman. As Thomas Merton once said, "To be a saint is to be myself." I need to be St. Anthony Cushing. I need to have faith for my life and respond to the Spirit in the situations that I find myself. I don't have to be a missionary in order for God to work mightily in my life. God can work a miracle in my family or at my job. For I know that what matters is not my own abilities but God's power. I am at least as inadequate as the frightened apostles of Pentecost morning; therefore, God can do great things in my life.

To have faith in my life is to be open to the Spirit in the ordinary situations I encounter. I noticed in my life that when I am faithful in the ordinary events of life, then I stumble into the miraculous from time to time. The miraculous usually happens when I am out on a limb or have made a mistake and generally have no way out but God's power (like the Israelites with their backs to the Red Sea).

Extraordinary situations of faith just seem to pop up. About four years ago I used to be really turned off by the over-emotional styles of some faith-healers. As a result I never laid hands on people and asked for a healing on the spot. However, one day in the college library, a friend in the community asked me to pray for her. She had a recently broken nose and a bad cold so that every time she'd sneeze or blow her nose it was agony. I said I'd pray and started to walk away and she said, "No, I want you to pray for me now. I can't stand this." So we prayed right there in the library. Almost immediately she went to wipe her nose and found out that all the pain was gone and when she looked in the mirror she saw that the bandage had puffed up when all the swelling had gone down. Strangely enough, while the Lord healed the broken nose she still had her cold. Anyway, this gave me a lot more faith to pray for healing and in the retreats and seminars we have run I've had to do that more and more and found out that the Lord really did heal people.

Another time a friend and I ended up evangelizing about twenty people in one night because our car broke down, and while we were waiting for someone to pick us up, we just started talking to people and had two prayer meetings right on the spot. It just seems that whenever you get to the point that the only thing you can do is have faith, then God does great things.

This happens over and over as people discover the kind of service that God wants them to do. One of the leaders and teachers in our community, Dan Thomson, used to be a tremendously shy person. For the first six months he was in the community, I hardly remember him saying anything at all, let alone suggesting anything for the community. One morning a few people who had leadership functions were having a discussion about how to arrange a communications system to keep in touch with the people in our teaching program. Just then Dan rushed in unaware of what we were discussing and blurted out, "I had this dream last night that the Lord wanted me to work out a communication system to keep in touch with people in the community." He got the job immediately. This particular job didn't last very long as the Lord began to use him very strongly in teaching and prophecy. He completely overcame his shyness and now is one of the most effective teachers and pastoral advisors in the community.

We've seen this kind of process happen over and over, though a little less dramatically. People who felt inadequate to the task took a risk in faith and found out that God did indeed use them. In the process their shyness and self-doubt would be healed so that the Lord could use them. God gives small, weak people great challenges, and his Spirit makes them great for the task. We are not capable of living the way Jesus lived, only the Spirit can do that in us.

Anytime I start to think of my abilities to do what the Lord wants, I start to get insecure. Who am I to teach people or write books? I have no credentials. Then as that insecurity drives me to prayer, I realize more and more that this is what God wants me to do. All I have to worry about is that I do what God wants. If that happens then what I do will work, not because I am special but because God has willed it. In this I find peace. Then, instead of spending my time worrying about my inadequacy, I am free to get on with the work the Lord has given me. As Cardinal Newman once said:

It is not giants who do most . . . Grace ever works by few, it is the keen vision, the intense conviction, the indomitable resolve of the few . . . it is the momentary crisis, it is the concentrated energy of a word or a look which is the instrument of heaven. Fear not little flock, for He is mighty who is in the midst of you and He will do for you great things. (*Lectures on the Present Position of Catholics in England: Addresses to the Brothers of the Oratory*)

Set your hearts on spiritual gifts (1 Corinthians 14:1).

Very often I hear people say that they aren't going to pursue the gifts of prophecy, tongues, healing, etc. because all they want is love. Often people think that this is the truly humble thing to do. They have gotten the impression that receiving gifts can quickly lead to a self-exalting pride. And this can happen if people associate gifts with holiness. However, Paul does not say that it is either love or spiritual gifts. It's *both* love *and* spiritual gifts. "Seek eagerly after love. Set your hearts on spiritual gifts" (1 Corinthians 14:1). Using spiritual gifts is a way of loving the people in the community. Since the motivation is love for others, we can ask for God to use us in all the different charisms. We are free to do this because we know that exercising the spiritual gifts is not a sign of holiness.

You can tell a tree by its fruit. None of those who cry out, "Lord, Lord" will enter the kingdom of God but only the one who does the will of my Father in heaven. When that day comes many will plead with me, "Lord, Lord, have we not prophesied in your name? Have we not exorcised demons by its power? Did we not do many miracles in your name as well?" Then I will declare to them solemnly, "I never knew you. Out of my sight, you evildoers" (Matthew 7:19-23).

It is not miraculous power, but love which is the true proof of holiness (1 Corinthians 13).

If we understand that love is what matters most and that the service gifts are neutral tools to be used for the sake of others, then denying gifts is a false notion of humility. Real humility is to recognize the truth of ourselves, our real goodness and real weakness. Humility is to do what God wants, not just what we think is humble. This subtle temptation to false humility is perfectly expressed in T.S. Eliot's *Murder in the Cathedral*. Thomas à Becket has renounced the temptations of power, wealth, and prestige only to encounter an unexpected devil who tries to persuade him that his desire for holiness is only spiritual pride, to be a great martyr in heaven. This temptation is to despair and cowardice because we think that anything else is "to do the right thing for the wrong reason."

I can humbly *seek* all the gifts of the Spirit for the sake of others. If God does not want me to exercise these gifts then no matter how much we seek them they won't be manifested in our life. Anyway, if all the humble people refuse to exercise the gifts then that leaves gifts for the proud to use. God will use those who are most open to the charisms. This is why many psychologically unbalanced people are so evident in the use of the charisms (authentic or not). Because God will use anyone, we see people with distorted notions of Christianity performing miracles because the well-balanced shy away from the extraordinary. A clear example is the ministry of deliverance. Most of the people I've seen exercising this gift have done so in a bizarre and alienating way. It is this kind of thing which further convinces the orthodox believer not to be open to this particular charism. As the process continues, many weak and trusting people end up going to groups on the fringes of Christianity because it's there that they find the power of God to meet their needs. It is not that all of these people are weird or heretical. If their churches were open to the gifts of the Spirit they might never have the need to leave. As it is, we often have the wrong people witnessing to the gifts of the Spirit, and this further increases the divisions in Christianity instead of healing them.

So if you want to be really humble, to be truly of service in a Christ-like way, seek to use the gifts of the Spirit in love. If you are afraid that this might be a temptation to pride, this might be a good indication that you will exercise the gifts without self-glorification but with "fear and trembling."

The reason I spent so much time on this whole topic of false humility is that I feel that one of the major reasons for the abuse of the charismatic gifts is that mature, balanced Christians refuse to be open to their operation. This is simply a question of strategy as to how to eliminate the abuse of the charisms. Other people would stress the need for humility in waiting instead of humility in seeking.

Now there is a constant danger of losing our perspective in seeking the gifts of the Spirit. It is a very real possibility that we might end up seeking the gifts instead of the giver, Jesus. Whenever we place our security in something other than God's love, we are running into trouble. The temptation with the gifts is that we start to think that we're worthwhile or special because we teach, prophesy or lead. We tend to find our security in what we do instead of who we are. Our worth comes from being loved not from exercising gifts. To say, "I have a ministry" is not to claim any credit but that of being a slave and lackey like Jesus. That we forget this from time to time is normal. How often do we fail to be totally dependent upon God? This is not the fault of the gifts of the Spirit; it's the fault of our weak and sinful personalities. People can find a false savior in motherhood or a career as well as prophecy and tongues, yet no one would suggest forsaking motherhood for humility's sake. Here I am talking about an attitude to our activities and service. We shouldn't avoid the gifts God is offering, but we can learn to accept them with the right perspective. This is the kind of balance expressed in the documents of Vatican II:

> The manifestation of the Spirit is given to everyone for profit. (1 Cor. 12:7) These charismatic gifts, whether they be the most outstanding or the more simple and widely diffused, are to be received with thanksgiving and consolation, for they are exceedingly suitable and useful for the needs of the church. Still, extraordinary gifts are not to be rashly sought after, nor are the fruits of apostolic labor to be presumptuously expected from them. In any case judgment as to their genuineness and proper use belongs to those who preside over the Church, and to whose special competence it belongs, not indeed to extinguish the Spirit, but to test all things and

hold fast to that which is good (cf. 1 Thess. 5:12, 19-21) (*Constitution on the Church*, p. 30).

DEVELOPING OUR GIFTS OF SERVICE

"To whom much is given much is expected" (Luke 12:18). I've been meditating on the Parable of the Talents and it terrifies me. I think Jesus could have been a lot more understanding about the man who buried his talents. After all, he was simply afraid to take a risk—that's normal. Jesus seemed to accept and forgive everything, even adultery. But what He tells the fearful servant is frightening.

> You worthless, lazy loat! You know I reap where I did not sow, and gather where I did not scatter. All the more reason to deposit my money with the bankers, so that on my return I could have had it back with interest. You there! Take the thousand away from him and give it to the man with 10,000. Those who have will get more until they grow rich while those who have not will lose even the little they have. Throw this worthless servant into the darkness outside, where he can wail and grind his teeth (Matthew 25:14-30).

The footnote in the New American Bible is more of an understatement than anything else: "The Christian community is . . . to function with a sense of personal responsibility for divine gifts received." I would have said something like "Watch Out! Don't slack off or play it safe. If you have any ability at all make sure you make the most of it! Don't worry about failure, just don't stagnate."

There is a real sense of reward in Jesus' attitude toward the people who worked with the gifts. He says, "Cleverly done! You are an industrious and reliable servant. Since you were dependable in a small matter, I will put you in charge of larger affairs. Come, share your master's joy" (Matthew 25:23).

It is interesting that there is no example of a servant who tried to work with his gift and failed. We would expect Jesus to say something to those of us who seem to try and try but never get anywhere in developing our gifts. Perhaps the reason for this omission is that *if we work with the gifts God has given us then we cannot fail in His eyes.* Success or failure just isn't part of God's categories. What He is concerned about is whether we are responsible or not.

All of us have talents and abilities that need to be transformed into gifts of service for the community. Whether it's prophecy or poetry we all need to respond to the Lord's call to responsibility for our gifts. Some of the qualities we found helpful in this were initiative, creativity and study.

INITIATIVE

Often people feel incapable of offering service to the community because they are not in a definite and structured ministry. Others wait for someone to ask them to do something important. Some wait for a direct revelation from God. And all the while there is plenty of work to be done to carry on the life of a Christian community. There is a need for a structured public ministry, but we should only have as much as we absolutely need. The rest of the work of the community can be left up to the initiative of the individual members.

This means that each Christian is to look actively for ways in which he can be of service to the community. There are dozens of "little things" to be done that make a community a place of warmth and love. Reaching out to new people, inviting them into our homes, listening to them, forming friendships, are all charismatic services that don't need a definite structure but subsist on spontaneous affection and love. A lot of this is anticipating each other's needs. Offering transportation, financial help, visiting the sick and lonely and imprisoned, having parties, are within the grasp of all of us. We don't need a special ordination to telephone someone to share what God is doing in our lives.

Another aspect of taking initiative to serve is simply asking the leadership what the needs of the community are. This is especially important in parish communities whose size prohibits an average person from knowing what the other parishioners need. Sometimes placing ourselves at the disposal of the pastor means that we get jobs that aren't really what we think are charismatic. Helping at Bingo, setting up socials or helping with the book work might not seem very spectacular but it is usually what the parish needs. This initiative also means communicating to the leadership what talents you do have and seeing if there is a place for them in the community. Some ideas are: artistic fields like painting, poetry or drama. Crafts—sewing, ceramics, carpentry, etc.; sports and entertainment, political and social action groups— all these are the rather humdrum things you'll find at any YMCA, but these are also the things that help create community.

In addition to this there are the services connected with worship and Christian education that are available to many in parishes and prayer groups. Taking initiative in these areas is first of all finding out what's involved in exercising a particular gift. For example, if you don't understand what prophecy is all about, call up someone who regularly exercises that gift and ask him about it. Generally it's good for people trying to involve themselves in a community to ask as many questions as possible. Part of this is a very important service gift of loving criticism. All I'm saying in all of this is that each person should actively look for ways to serve the community.

STUDY AND CREATIVITY

The responsibility to study to prepare ourselves for service is first of all a willingness to learn from others how to serve. This is particularly true of Christian education. We need to know what the Church actually teaches, how the Spirit has worked in the lives of the saints and Church tradition. All of this gives us a sense of perspective and gives us a challenge to sainthood that our contemporaries often fail to provide. This means we must be willing to have our horizons broadened, to be stretched, to be willing to admit our limitations. For those involved in the Charismatic Renewal this implies that we are open to hear what the Spirit is saying in renewals other than that of Pentecostalism. It also says that we should be particularly responsive to criticism to see if there is anything we could be doing better (and there always is). There are prophetic voices, loving communities, and gifts of wisdom and service outside the Charismatic Renewal that the renewal needs to hear if it is to mature into something both holy and human. (In some areas like marriage authority, social action, and liturgy the renewal is still too new and too narrow to have great theological depth in these areas. It's okay to be there, we are still growing. But we still need to study how the Spirit has led other groups like the Focolare, Marriage Encounter, Catholic-Worker Movement, the Liturgical Renewal, to hear how the insights of the Charismatic Renewal can be integrated into the life of the Church.)

Very often our study gives us a push to be creative in service. Spiritual maturity is human maturity, and this means developing our potential and talents to the fullest. It's sad to see how so many people in our culture have stagnated in the atmosphere of instant foods and TV. Sometimes I'll ask the people in our seminars, "What do you like to do?" and most of them either don't know what they like or never seem to find the time for it. Our creativity has been deadened and many need a kind of psychological healing to take once again the risk to be playful, wonder-full, creative children of God. So, explore all the possibilities and try to discover your special gift. Usually we are only creative at what we really like to do. Maybe you always wanted to act, write, be a gourmet cook, paint, be a fantastic gardener. Whatever it is let God's Spirit help you share in the creativity of God. This is a gift both to yourself and to the community. Most of the time there won't be an official structure for these kinds of activities. Here each person's creativity challenges the leadership to help them develop their talents. Just recently, for example, we've been trying to get an art center going to give people a forum to develop these talents. Already a coffeehouse initiated by someone not even in the community provides a setting for music, drama, poetry, and games. If these kinds of structures can't be developed, people can still pursue their talents individually and in guild-type small groups. It is not unspiritual to re-create ourselves through art and hobbies. It is basic to what the Incarnation means to let the Spirit work in every aspect of our lives.

DISCERNING OUR GIFTS

The most frequently asked question about the gifts of service is, "How do I know what my particular gift is?" In movies, books, and our everyday life, we see strange and usually sincere people setting themselves up as prophets, healers, or teachers. And as we grow closer to God we see more clearly our capacity to deceive ourselves and to "do the right thing for the wrong reason." How do I know then what my special gift is for the community? Should I just wait for someone to ask me to do something? Should I volunteer?

The best way we've found to discern a person's particular gift is taken from Arnold Bittlinger's book *Gifts and Graces*. There are three elements to discerning a gift for the community:

1. inner call,
2. community discernment,
3. the fruit that particular gift produces.

INNER CALL

This simply means that a person will sense in prayer that God wants him to get involved in a particular activity. This is what St. Ignatius would call consolation. "The peace that Christ gives is to be the judge in your hearts: for to this peace God has called you together in one body" (Colossians 3:15, TEV). We sense God's presence in a particular activity. We feel peaceful about doing it. We still might be nervous or feel inadequate, but deep down there's a feeling of rightness that the Spirit gives us. Secondly, each of us has normal desires and inclinations. We enjoy teaching or painting, cooking, exercising, hospitality, etc., and in some way this is an indication that God has made us for a particular task. Most of the time I would think that our major service is something we should find easy to do. The pastor of our parish is this kind of person. He always wanted to be a priest; he likes the work; never feels bored and generally is in a good mood about it all. As the Psalmist says, "Delight in the Lord and He will give you your heart's desire."

Having an inner peace and calling from God is not necessarily something spectacular. Once in a while someone might have a vision or dream about his or her service, but usually we sense the "still small voice" of God within us. If something more dramatic does happen this is no cause for great concern. We need to "test all things and hold on to what is good" (1 Thessalonians 5). For example, St. Francis de Sales had a vision of three women coming to him to start a religious order. He trusted in God, continued to work at his everyday responsibilities and *ten years later* the order was founded.

COMMUNITY DISCERNMENT

The group of believers was one in mind and heart (Acts 2:32).

Because the gifts of service are for the community they are to be discerned by the community. Usually this happens through the leadership of a prayer group and ultimately through the Church authority. This is done that all services might be coordinated in love. Also, it helps to have community discernment to free us from any tendency to self-delusion.

The community leadership should discern whom they want to perform particular jobs and how they would want it carried out. In our community this is done in a very informal way with those in charge of each particular service. We have a task-oriented leadership that works on the principle of subsidiarity. For example, if someone feels a call to get involved with the teaching program, he talks to the teaching coordinator. Neither the whole community nor the whole leadership group needs to make a decision on this level. Just trust each of the leaders of the services to discern who should be involved in that particular service.

It is very rare that we will turn down a person who wants to get involved in a service. Usually we treat these things with a very experimental "give it a try" attitude. The leadership is there to facilitate discernment and most people can't discern something until they've given it a try at least. With more public services we take a bit more care to insure that the people involved are witnesses to love and freedom.

If a person is turned down for a particular service it is usually to redirect them into something else. People have a tendency to get involved in the more public services like teaching, simply because they are unaware of anything else they could be doing for the community. This reflects a healthy desire to do something for the community, but often it is not a sense of calling in prayer but simply a good idea. Talking and praying together can help the person authentically discern where his talents are and direct him to a mutually satisfying service.

There are times when the leadership needs to take the initiative in encouraging people to a particular service. This was especially true in terms of women teaching in our seminar program. Although we had made it clear that both women and men could teach the seminars, it happened that only a few women volunteered. By and large they felt inadequate for teaching with the result that women made up 90% of our small group leaders but only 10% of our teachers. We saw that we had to counteract the sickness in our culture that makes many women feel inadequate in leadership. So we had to go out of our way not only to offer but consciously encourage and work with the women to overcome this hesitance to teach.

The sense of community discernment is both a prayerful seeking of God's will and simple coordination of work. The communal sense of God's will is most evident in response to word gifts in prayer meetings and in communal decision making. If a person feels that he has a ministry of prophecy for a community and the community consistently feels that he doesn't, then that person should try serving the community in some other way. The same thing applies to projects offered to the community. An individual cannot always expect the community to support her or him in a project that calls for commitment of time and resources from a lot of people. There are practical demands made on a community that need to be fulfilled with regularity. People have to teach, lead, take care of the physical needs for a group. These need to be coordinated with responsibility so that people can be served. To fail to set up the chairs for a meeting because you feel that the Lord leads you to prophesy to someone is a very unloving inspiration. This is a simple task of being where you're needed when you're needed. Suppose someone wants to start a house of prayer or a social action project. If the community discerns that God is leading them to something else, then the practical limitation of time and resources almost demands that a very good project like a house of prayer cannot be embraced. One could then go ahead and try this on one's own, or if one feels very strongly about this, one could go to a community that is interested in developing a house of prayer. This is just to say that each particular community cannot embrace all the possible services of the universal Church. Here the freedom of each individual needs to be balanced by the responsibilities of service to the Church. Again there is a beautifully balanced statement in the Vatican documents:

> For the exercise of this apostolate, the Holy Spirit, who sanctifies the People of God through the ministry and the sacraments, gives to the faithful special gifts as well (Cf. 1 Corinthians 12:7) "allotting to everyone according as he will" (1 Corinthians 12:11). Thus may the individuals, "according to the gift that each has received, administer it to one another" and become "good stewards of the manifold grace of God" (1 Peter 4:10) and build up thereby the whole body in charity (Cf. Ephesians 4:10). From the reception of these gifts, including those which are less dramatic, there arise for each believer the right and duty to use them in the Church and in the world for the good of mankind and for the upbuilding of the Church. In so doing, believers need to enjoy the freedom of the Holy Spirit who "breathes where he wills" (John 3:8). At the same time, they must act in communion with their brothers in Christ, especially with their pastors. The latter must make a judgment about the true nature and proper use of these gifts, not in order to extinguish the Spirit, but to test all things and hold fast to what is good (cf. 1 Thessalonians 5:12, 19, 21) (*Decree on the Apostolate of the Laity*, pp. 492-493).

THE FRUITS OF SERVICE

To each person the manifestation of the Spirit is given for the common good (1 Corinthians 12:7).

By their fruits you shall know them (Matthew 7:20).

This is the ultimate test of any gift or service for the community. Obviously this happens after a gift has already been exercised. This is the only true discernment for some gifts that are permanent. I mean, how can you discern the authenticity of marriage or martyrdom until after the fact. As to marriage and its discernment one would wish for God to once again start writing on the wall. The gifts of the Spirit actually change the Church, bringing about love, joy, peace, and unity. This means that prophecy actually brings people to repentance. In physical services the job simply gets done as lovingly and efficiently as possible. For example, the man who takes care of the setup for our open meeting does such a good job that many people simply take it for granted that this will happen every week. That is real faithfulness.

This discernment is the qualitative evaluation of the work of the Spirit in the community and the person giving the service. This takes time and a lot of honesty. A person might feel led to a certain ministry and the community concurs. But if after a period of time there is no apparent benefit for the people being served then maybe that person should try something else. The opposite case is also true: there may be great benefit from a person's service but if that person isn't growing then he should probably be allowed to look elsewhere. The reason for this is that the gifts of the Spirit are intended to be "sanctifying gifts." They are to lead a person closer to God through personal satisfaction and affirmation as well as through occasional suffering. If a person continually feels oppressed and alienated by his service then chances are that that is not the service for him. And the community should not attempt to coerce a person to remain in a position that is destructive to his or her life with God. There are many qualifications to this. A person might need psychological healing or more support or perhaps is just having an attack of laziness. Writing is sometimes excruciating for me. Organizational work is always an agony. That is just a problem with my personality that I need to endure and grow through. However, on the whole, I feel that my work is truly making me more free and loving.

DISCERNMENT IN CHURCH HISTORY

Sometimes discerning the fruit of a person's service is a very complicated affair. For the Catholic Church there is a tradition of quiet unassuming service which is very often so humble as to go unnoticed. Many great saints (Ignatius, John of the Cross) were opposed by some Church authorities during their lifetimes. John

Bosco's superior tried to have him put in an insane asylum. Many others lives of heroism and service were only recognized after their death. For example Charles de Foucauld felt called to be a missionary and spent 12 years in Morocco without making one convert! However, his life and spirituality gathered together a group of men and women (Little Brothers and Sisters of Jesus) whose life of radical service is one of the great witnesses of the modern Church.

In terms of prophecy, visions, and spiritualities, discernment of the fruits of these gifts must stand the tests of time and authority. Recently there have been scores of Marian prophecies but only a few have been discerned as authentic. No one can discern someone else's vision or apparition to have actually happened because no one can tell for sure what another person is experiencing. There can be a sense of consolation experienced as when a prophecy is given. You can analyze the content of the message according to Scripture and Tradition, and then look at the fruits of holiness in the person who has the vision, etc., and the followers of that spirituality. This is what the Church has done with the visions at Lourdes and Fatima. The Church discerned that there is nothing contrary to the faith in the visions. It does not say that this spirituality is better than any other. It just says that a person can follow this and still be faithful to the Church. There are other cases where the prophetic messages of obviously holy people have been seen as false. For example, when St. Catherine of Siena, a Doctor of the Church, had an apparition where the Virgin Mary told her that she was not the Immaculate Conception; or, in terms of prophecy not coming to pass, as when St. Vincent Ferrer was convinced that all of his miracles were signs that the second coming was due before his death.

Having a sense of history about how the Spirit has worked in the lives of the saints has a liberating effect on our service. First of all, we see that the Lord used all kinds of people, some strong and intelligent, others weak, ignorant, and moody. Many of them seemed to be failures. My namesake, Anthony of Padua, failed in joining a couple of religious orders before he finally made it with the Franciscans. Few of the saints were predictable, and often it was the great saints who most upset the established ways of their communities. Many had glaring weaknesses and strange idiosyncrasies. This is what we see happening in our community. Weak people are being used by God to carry on His work.

Thus, when you think of "what my gift is for the community," you have the basic guidelines of inner call, community discernment and fruits of that gift. There are some other attitudes that help us to have faith.

The first is to have an attitude of flexibility and experimentation. We must be able to read "the signs of the times" and move as the Spirit directs us to meet the needs of modern men.

This means that we should be *non-possessive* about the kind of service we are doing for the Church. There is no such thing as *my gift*. The gifts are for the Church community. We might really be attached to the idea of being a teacher, healer, or someone "who loves to be their leader" (3 John 1:9 TEV). We must be always ready to renounce our normal service to meet the present needs of the Church. We need the flexibility to change, to realize that God might want to use us in a particular service only for a short time. We might be called on to change the particular style of our service. For example, what I most enjoy doing for the community is praying for healing. However, to find time to write, I've had to cut down on praying for healing. This flexibility applies to communities and whole movements also, as one day the Charismatic Renewal will have to die to itself and bring its life to the Church.

RESPONSIBILITY

There is a legitimate need for order and efficiency in a community, but this is always coordinated with sensitivity to personal needs. Faithfulness is a fruit of the spirit and it doesn't grow up overnight. Almost all of the services in our community began with lots of mistakes, failures, and irresponsibility. It takes most people a good while to learn how to serve in a community. Thank God our leader had enough wisdom and patience to keep on giving people another chance. Working for a community should be different from working in a factory. There is room for forgiveness and understanding. Community should be the place where you can "fail gracefully." So as new people enter the service of the community we must give them the same chance to make mistakes that we had. Our normal desire for productivity needs to be balanced by tolerance for where people are with God.

MOTIVATION

Occasionally people get worried about their motives for getting involved in service. They feel that they easily succumb to their desire to feel important and to be the center of attention. Realistically, we all know people who seem to use the gifts of the Spirit as signs of self-importance. Well, to tell the truth, I easily succumbed to my need to be the center of attention. I think all of us need recognition, need to feel important. We almost never have a consciously bad motive. Those are easy to deal with. However, usually I can never discern bad motivations simply by introspecting. My subconscious is clever enough to mask any desire for self-glorification behind pious intentions.

I normally assume that I have mixed motivations for anything I do. I desire to serve people by teaching and writing, but I also enjoy the praise as much as I try to avoid it.

What I find does happen is that as I am working in a particular service I discover bad motivations as a result of prayer, love, and honesty. So, if you are worried about why you're doing something, trust that consciously you're trying to love. Anything else will come out organically as you grow in the Lord. If God could use a jackass to prophesy (Numbers 2:11), he could easily use us with our mixed motives.

WHAT CAN HAPPEN

God is always at work in you to make you willing and able to obey his own purpose (Philippians 2:12 TEV).

One of the greatest insights of the Charismatic Movement is that God's Spirit works in every Christian regardless of age, education or credentials. "God chose those whom the world considers absurd to shame the wise; he singled out the weak of this world to shame the strong" (1 Corinthians 2:27). God will use us, weak as we are, to change His church and world.

What we have seen happen in our parish and the covenant

community is a verification that God will use ordinary people to complete His work. People who were once crippled with shyness are now witnessing in front of hundreds. Others who were immersed in the middle class trap are opening up their homes to strangers and sharing their wealth with those in need. In the parish, the faithful service of the Director of Religious Education and the CCD teachers has brought catechetics back into the home; families are praying together again; and about 200 people have been brought back to the Church through this program. In the last 5 years, the conversion classes have grown from 4 to 80 people. During this time the income of the parish has gone up 2 ½ times. An example is a girl making $5,000 a year who four years ago used to give about $50.00 a year to the church and has gradually felt led to contribute more and more to where she now gives over $1,500.00 a year to the parish. The renewal of faith has led to an enlivened liturgy and a new choir, a school faculty who prays together, and a lay ministry to the sick. The 80 people in the covenant community have helped start about 25 other groups and have run retreats and workshops for about 20,000 people in the last four years. Many of the members are involved in social service jobs and also serve in other parishes and social programs.

All of us have a clear sense that this is only the beginning. We anticipate 10 years for the renewal of the parish. We are excited at all that God has done among us and can only pray

> To him who is able to do so much more than we can ever ask for or even think of, by means of the power working in us: to God be the glory in the Church and in Christ Jesus, for all time, for ever and ever! Amen. (Ephesians 3:20-21—TEV)

BIBLIOGRAPHY

RECOMMENDED READING:

Bittlinger, Arnold, *Gifts and Graces: A Commentary on 1 Corinthians 12-14*, William B. Eerdmans Publishing Co., Grand Rapids, Michigan, 1967, 126 pp.
A rather complete study of the nature and function of

the charismatic gifts. Most balanced, theologically sound, yet experience-oriented book I've read on the charisms.

Haughey, John C., S.J., *The Conspiracy of God: The Holy Spirit in Men*, Doubleday & Co., Garden City, New York, 1973, 154 pp.

Great for understanding the person of the Holy Spirit and the quality of man's response. Focuses on the Spirit in the life of Jesus.

McDonnell, Killian, O.S.B., and Bittlinger, Arnold, *The Baptism in the Holy Spirit as an Ecumenical Problem* (Two Essays Relating the Baptism in the Holy Spirit to the Sacramental Life), Charismatic Renewal Services, Notre Dame, Indiana, 1972, 53 pp.

Good for relating the pentecostal experience to a more traditional theology. Especially relevant to this chapter is McDonnell's treatment of the charisms.

SUPPLEMENTARY READING:

Bittlinger, Arnold, *Gifts and Ministries*, William B. Eerdmans Publishing Co., Grand Rapids, Michigan, 1973, 109 pp.

Again Bittlinger does a thorough exegesis on the scriptural basis for charisms and the ministries in the body of Christ. The focus is on integrating charismatic gifts with the institutional offices and ministries.

Hyde, Douglas, *Dedication and Leadership*, University of Notre Dame Press, Notre Dame, Indiana, 1966, 158 pp.

Mr. Hyde was a leader in the British Communist party for 20 years before he converted to Catholicism. This book describes the organizational techniques that help the Communists to have such a large impact on society. In this, he challenges Catholics to take what is good from the communists to increase our dedication to the truth.

Theological and Pastoral Orientations on the Catholic Charismatic Renewal, The Word of Life, Notre Dame, Indiana, 1974, 71 pp.

This is a paper prepared by an international group of charismatic leaders and theologians describing a Catholic perspective on the Charismatic Renewal. It is very good in terms of integration with the broader life of the Church.

by Joseph Lange

Authority 2

"I can't wait till I grow up. Then I'll do whatever I want."

"As long as you live in this house and I'm your mother, you'll do what you're told."

"Every time I see a policeman, I feel like he might pull me over for some violation or other."

"If the boss says do it, you do it."

As we grow up, we encounter authority in a variety of forms and from a variety of sources. Parents (and sometimes brothers, sisters and assorted relatives) tell us what to do. Babysitters, teachers, and other "older" people command us. Bigger "kids" sometimes made us afraid or even forced us to do things by an advantage of strength. We experienced police, perhaps the army, and government regulations as coercive.

We use the word "authority" to describe a number of relationships, as is clear from what was just said. Perhaps it would be worthwhile to spell that out in more detail.

1. Parents exercise authority over their children in order to bring them to maturity. How the authority is exercised varies from society to society, but it usually amounts to the power to give orders and expect them to be obeyed. That does not describe the whole relationship, but our topic is authority. Children experience authority as coercion or as the need to ask permission.

2. Governments exercise authority through laws and officials. Obedience is expected, of course. We have become used to that.

3. In work situations the "boss" makes decisions and those under him are expected to carry them out.

4. There's an authority, too, which comes from "being in relation to the author." It is not experienced as coercive, but as

something which gives confidence. During the sixties in this country a lot of things were going on which were clearly at odds with what we claim this country is about. We seemed to be fighting an unjust war, minorities were being oppressed, all men were not being treated equally. Political officials continued to wield power, but they lost their "authority" in the sense we are talking about.

5. Then there is the authority of expertise, of the one who is an "authority on the subject." He is listened to because he knows what he is talking about.

6. And, finally, there is the authority of the truth. The one who speaks the truth, the one who lives the truth commands attention because that is the way truth works. It is not coercive authority, but when you hear or experience the truth about yourself, about the meaning of life, about anything, you know you ignore its demands only at your own peril.

Our experience of authority in the first three cases, however reasonable and just, is related to the exercise of power. The power may come from an office, from money, or from might, but power it is. Our feelings and ideas about authority are absorbed as part of our growing up in the world, and, as with everything else, we must examine those ideas and feelings in the light of the Gospel.

THE TEACHING OF JESUS

Jesus had some things to say about how people should relate to each other. We already know that He commands us to love one another as He has loved us. That puts a lot of demands on us, but it does not seem to solve the problem of parents or officials in the community of the followers of Jesus, the Church. We are commanded to be brother and sister to each other in love, but the question is: Is there also a relationship of submission of superior to inferior, of leader to subordinate in Jesus' vision of our life together?

Let us begin with the clearest statement of Jesus on rank and position and then fill in the picture with His other sayings and actions.

In Matthew 20:20-28, Mark 10:35-45, and Luke 22:24-27 Jesus deals explicitly with the question of leadership:

When the other ten heard this then began to feel indignant with James and John, so Jesus called them to him and said to them: "You know that among the pagans their so-called rulers lord it over them, and their great men make their authority felt. This is not to happen among you. No; anyone who wants to become great among you must be your servant, and anyone who wants to be first among you must be slave to all. For the Son of Man himself did not come to be served but to serve, and to give his life as a ransom for many" (Mark—JB).

It could not be any clearer. Jesus makes very plain that our life together is to be radically different from that of the pagans. There is to be no lording over one another as the pagans do. Whoever assumes the role of leadership is not to consider himself lord and master. Instead he is to be a slave, a deacon, a lackey, a menial, one who serves.

In John's Gospel Jesus makes the same point by the episode of washing the feet of the disciples.

When he had washed their feet and put on his clothes again he went back to the table. "Do you understand," he said, "what I have done to you? You call me Master and Lord, and rightly; so I am. If I, then, the Lord and Master have washed your feet, you should wash each other's feet. I have given you an example so that you may copy what I have done to you. I tell you most solemnly, no servant is greater than his master, no messenger is greater than the one who sent him" (John 13:12-16).

In John's Gospel, too, we find Jesus using the image of the shepherd (10:11-18). In the Near East writings and in the Old Testament, "shepherd" was a regal title. Jesus did accept the title of "king," too, but He qualifies it: because He is shepherd and king He has authority to lay down His life.

He also has the authority (*exousia*) to teach, and his authority comes from the Father. Jesus does what the Father does, does only the will of the Father. His authority rests on obedience to God alone.

All through His public life Jesus had to struggle with the problems of being the Messiah-King. The people were used to thinking and feeling about authority as we are. They looked for a Son of David who would act like another worldly king. But Jesus was about to do something else. He wanted a kingdom of love.

He also had the problem of proclaiming the new Kingdom of God in a way that would not coerce. From the temptations at the beginning to the taunts when He was on the cross, "Come down from the cross and we will believe you," He was tempted to use His power in a way that would compel belief. But He would not use it that way. Jesus invites, He does not force.

In another way Jesus points out the way we should feel about ourselves. In Matthew 18:1-5, Mark 9:33-37, and Luke 9:46-48, He uses the image of a child and says, "For the least among you all, that is the one who is great" (Luke 9:48—JB).

Lackeys (deacons) and children are people who are subject to the will of another. It could not be more plain. Jesus wants us to see that in His kingdom things are to be much different from anything we experience in the world. There is to be no lording it over, no distinctions, no coercion. The community of His followers is not to be modeled on the communities of the world.

Jesus' life builds to His death, His laying down His life for us. In the end He calls us "not servants, but friends," and He promises us the Spirit so that we can do as He does, love as He loves.

Finally, before Pilate, Jesus acknowledges publicly that He is king: "Yes, I am a king. I was born for this, I came into the world for this: to bear witness to the truth; and all who are on the side of truth listen to my voice" (John 18:37—JB). This is the ultimate experience of the authority of Jesus: He proclaims the truth to us, the truth about ourselves, the truth about life and death and resurrection, the truth about the Father and love and peace and joy, the truth about all of human life. In the end, Jesus is Himself the Truth.

Accepting Jesus as our only Savior and our only Lord is accepting the whole Truth. Becoming like Jesus through the power of the Spirit is to come into the light where things can be seen for what they are. The authority of the truth unclouded by coercion or prestige speaks to the heart of those who are "on the side of Truth," and that authority is from the Father, for it is His Truth that is incarnate in Jesus, who came to be and do and say only what the Father gives Him.

The authority of Jesus operates on the truth that a response which is the result of coercion excludes the response that can be given from freely chosen love. And Jesus both commands us to love and sets us free. "So if the Son makes you free, you will be free indeed" (John 8:36—JB). Jesus merely proclaims and offers the truth. The people said He spoke with authority (*exousia*). He leaves us free to say Yes or No.

It should also be noted that the gospels speak to us as clearly by what they do not say as by what they say. There were many, many ways that Jesus could have spoken of his followers ruling with mercy and justice. He had the language and the images available to Him. The fact that He did not in any way speak about these things, but, instead, told us explicitly that we are not to think of authority as the pagans do, should say to us once and for all that Jesus came to lead us to a new way of living together. We just have to get used to that.

Finally, Jesus commissioned the Apostles as He was com-missioned by the Father to carry on His mission. Henceforth theirs would be the authority in the power of the Spirit to speak the truth in love, to teach, to heal and deliver, to baptize. This becomes the mission of the Church, of God's people. It is the whole Church which continues the mission. Jesus Himself is still with us and He alone is the head of His Church.

The vision of Jesus, then, is for all men to become as little children and slaves of each other, living in the power of the truth in love for one another, setting each other free.

THE EXPERIENCE OF THE APOSTOLIC CHURCH

The behavior of the Apostles indicates that they had learned their lesson well from Jesus and the Spirit. No one denies that Peter exercised a leadership role, often as spokesman for the rest, but it is also clear that Peter never acted independently of the others.

As converts were made and the first Jerusalem community

began to form, it seems as though the Apostles assumed the role of caring for the distributions of goods (Acts 5). Then, when problems with that developed, "the Twelve called a full meeting of the disciples and addressed them" (Acts 6). They called for others to be selected for that task so that they could continue to devote themselves to "prayer and to the service of the Word." The whole assembly approved and selected seven men. The Apostles prayed and laid hands on them.

This is really instructive because we see the Apostles indicating their own understanding of their commission and we also see the community acting together in the selection of its new officers. We see as well that this new office grew naturally out of the needs of people living together.

The Apostles saw themselves as men who needed to pray, to be with God that they might know Him and know His will. They also understood that their authority lay in their "service to the Word." They did not act independently of their brothers and sisters, lording it over them, or, more subtly, directing them. Instead, they did as Jesus did.

The community itself took up its own exercise of authority by selecting the deacons (lackeys!). The point here is a simple one: if people are going to live together in some sort of community, the life of the community will demand some order and some officers. Jesus did not seem to bother about some once-and-for-all form or structure. Rather, He indicated the principles by which a structure and offices should be chosen and operated: love, freedom, service, and truth. He remains, He lives on as *the* Head of the Church and His Spirit is given to guide in the development of the Church. Obviously, Christians have not always implemented the teaching of Jesus in their structures, but once again we are given a chance to repent and start over.

The Apostolic Church knew no set or frozen form. Instead we see a gradual development of offices and structures under the guidance of the Spirit. Gradually other offices are added such as pastor, teacher, overseer (bishop), and presbyter. What is vital to see here is that the particular structure and offices are not at all important or fixed. What is important is that the Christian community operate as brothers and sisters who love and trust one another, set each other free, and live in the Truth. That is a bit of a job, isn't it?

Another example of the way in which authority resides in the community, the Church, can be seen in the crisis caused by the conversion of pagans. You remember Peter's vision and visit with Cornelius. While Peter was speaking, the Spirit came upon all in the house of Cornelius (Acts 10). Peter had to justify himself to the rest at Jerusalem, and after pagans everywhere began to be filled with the Spirit, the matter was taken up in Jerusalem again. Whether there was an actual assembly or a series of informal discussions, which Luke presents as an assembly for the sake of convenience, we do not know. It does not matter.

We need to appreciate the immensity of the problem as the people saw it then. The Apostles and the first Jewish converts were annoyed that non-Jews were receiving the Spirit. Jesus had ministered only to the Jews, had picked only Jews to be His Apostles, and at first the Apostles had no idea that they would be breaking away from Judaism and the Law. Now they were asked to face the fact that the Lord was calling Gentiles to Himself without any reference to the Law. This meant sharing with "brothers and sisters" who were uncircumcised, and such everyday things as becoming "defiled" by eating forbidden foods.

The Christian people had become international and interracial. What would be the consequences of abandoning the Law and identity with God's chosen people? The stakes were high. I believe it is of immense significance that the decision in this crisis was not made on the basis of possible consequences, but on the *source* of the change. Because it was of the Spirit we accept it. Period. The function of the Apostles and the community in this crisis was to discover the truth of what God was about. "Discernment" is a good word here: to discover the will of God.

The results of the decision, of course, were not uniformly accepted. People followed Paul everywhere trying to undermine His authority (service of the Word) and trying to get the Gentile converts to accept the Law. The lesson in this is that not all of us hear and accept all of the Good News all at once. Though everyone had the Spirit, not even in the Apostolic Church did the presence of the Spirit protect everyone from error and dissension.

So far we have seen the practice of the Apostles and the Apostolic Church. While the forms changed and developed, they remained true to the principles of Jesus even to letting go of the Law.

It would be possible to go into this much more extensively, but I do not think we need to do that. Instead, let us turn to Paul. In the July 1972 issue of *The Way* (Vol. 12, No. 3, pp. 220-221), there is an article, "Authority in the Gospel," by John Ashton. In that article he says of Paul:

The paradigm case of the apostle, the missioner entrusted with the message of reconciliation, is St. Paul. As we know, he had at first thought of commending this message to the Corinthians by a display of "lofty words and wisdom" (the intellectual's form of the temptation that confronted Christ on the pinnacle of the temple. And if, as is possible, he did in fact yield to this temptation at Athens, he soon became aware that this kind of preaching, resting on personal prestige and authority, could not win for Christ the sort of allegiance he sought. So it was that his speech and his message to the Corinthians were not in plausible words of wisdom, but in the demonstration of the Spirit and power, that your faith might not rest in the wisdom of men but in the power of God! (The Spirit, of course, *is* the power of God—power being a word Paul is not afraid of using in this context; and the power of God has been identified earlier with "the word of the cross.") Later, reflecting on the nature of his vision as an apostle, he made a further statement of policy: "We have renounced disgraceful, underhanded ways; we refuse to practice cunning or to tamper with God's word, but by the open statement of the truth we could commend ourselves to every man's conscience in the sight of God!" The Truth must be allowed to make its own appeal to the free human conscience, and the joy of the apostle is to insure that the voice of Christ is not muffled by his own claims to prestige and privilege, and the cross of Christ not overshadowed by his own posturings. Hence the severe warnings to those in authority in the pastoral epistles. It is easy for the servant to dress up in the robes of authority, and so stifle the Spirit, and deprive the message of its true power.

To Paul we are also indebted for the image of the Body of Christ. In response to problems of order in Corinth Paul reminds the Corinthians that though there are many different gifts and services, there is only one Lord and one Spirit. All of us make up one Body with Jesus as the head. One position is not greater than the other. There is one Spirit. Then follows the great hymn to love whose whole point is that each one with some gift or service for the life of the community must so live that everything be coordinated in love. There is for Paul no division between church leaders and the laity. We are one Body. There is only one Spirit. The authority and the power reside in the whole Body, not in any special individual or group. Let us close this section with the words from Ephesians (4:11-16):

> And to some, his gift was that they should be apostles; to some, prophets; to some, evangelists; to some, pastors and teachers; so that the saints together make a unity in the work of service, building up the body of Christ. In this way we are all to come to unity in our faith and in our knowledge of the Son of God, until we become the perfect Man, fully mature with the fullness of Christ himself.

> . . . . If we live by the truth and in love, we shall grow in all ways into Christ, who is the head by whom the whole body is fitted and joined together, every joint adding its own strength, for each separate part to work according to its function. So the body grows until it has built itself up, in love.

THE CONSEQUENCES FOR US

Our first response to the word of Jesus must be repentance. His truth casts light on our folly and we stand convicted. We need to change in our attitudes, our behaviors and our structures until we grow into the fullness of Christ.

Over the centuries, for a variety of reasons, our poor Church has been burdened with the trappings of worldly power and authority. It is no easy task to shed the image of worldly office and power or to hold the entirely new idea of the Church community in one's mind while encountering the worldly model everywhere else. It is certainly not easy to call people to freedom without coercion and not intervene "for their own good."

And so we have ranks and titles and prestige and the misuse of power. We have talk of obedience and submission and headship. So be it. We need to repent. We can only thank God that He has again sent prophets to proclaim the truth and to call us to repentance.

Still, the other side of the coin needs to be displayed so that our image will not be distorted. Along with sin and fault there has been heroism and love and sacrifice. The message of Jesus has been proclaimed, the Bible preserved, the sacraments celebrated, men and women sanctified.

If the truth is to be faced, then we must all assume the guilt together. Authority is given to the whole Church, not to just a few. We have not spoken the truth in love; we have treated offices of the Church as if they were special, in ways that confirm a mistaken notion of authority; we have not contributed our gift to the life of the Body; we have not loved the Church, not really.

Our task now is not to run around pointing our finger at bishops and priests, judging them and condemning them. The problem facing them and us is much too complex for that to do any good anyhow. Instead, we begin with ourselves. We look at our own attitudes and feelings toward authority. We look at our own behavior toward authority.

It is not uncommon for people joining our community to be afraid of me or to be unduly respectful. I am a priest and a leader of this community and people bring with them the attitudes of the world toward leaders. Nothing in the world tends to make a man feel more powerful than to be treated as someone special. The feelings of fear and the behavior of special treatment must be repented of. It is a humble place to start, but it is in keeping with where we are.

We can also begin to look with new eyes and hearts at the beauty of our Church. Leaving all negativism behind, we can begin to wonder at the presence of Jesus in the teaching and actions of the Church. We can learn to love her. We can learn to build her up by our work and our actions. This does not mean that there is not a time and a place for loving criticism; but it does mean that more is accomplished by building up than by tearing down, and it means that the Lord will provide the right time and place for criticism. As we change, the Church changes, because we are the Church.

In terms of our attitudes toward ourselves, we must begin to think of ourselves as bearing a gift for the life of the Church. The authority of Jesus is given to the whole Church, which means that we share in the mission to speak the truth in love, to heal, to drive out demons, to forgive, to love, and to serve. So much is said about authority meaning service today, and we are so used to looking at a small number of people holding offices in the Church that we forget that we are called to exercise that authority of service. Everyone is called to serve everyone else in the Body as love demands. We are all brothers and sisters to each other.

Practically, it is probably not a good idea to run to our pastors and bishops and declare that we have been given a gift of prophecy (or something like that) and demand an opportunity at Mass to speak God's word to His people. Let us seek the Lord's time and the Lord's way. Let us not get ahead of Him. If we keep our eyes and ears open, we will see the Lord leading us into service.

It's so important to realize that there is no place in the Body of Christ for power relationships. Since Jesus alone is the Head of the Church, the most important question in all that we do together is: What does the Lord want? To bring that question to church meetings of every sort is to eliminate division and power struggles. It is prophetic.

THE ROLE OF WOMEN IN THE CHURCH

This is not the place to go into an extensive treatment of this subject. See the reading list at the end of this chapter and the Appendix. Those who are already convinced that women have equal rights as children of God need no more than the following. Those who are not convinced will need more than this context will allow.

It took Christianity 19 centuries to acknowledge the evil of slavery. In the 20th century we are beginning to admit the truth of the full rights of women. There is no *sound* scriptural base for the second-class role assigned to women, though literalist (and wrong) interpretations of Paul abound. I know that in saying this I am opposing a lot of other Christian teachers, but the truth is out! The Spirit is given to all men and women, and there are no distinctions among the followers of Jesus.

The fact that the majority of teachers in Christendom over the past 100 years have been women says something about their already being in possession of a lot of the authority of Jesus. The fight over women's roles has already been fought in some measure in the Roman Church prior to naming Teresa of Avila and Catherine of Siena as Doctors of the Church. In fact, it is absurd to believe that women who can be presidents of universities and competent in every field of life must be excluded from other positions of responsibility in the Church. The truth is out.

In our own community we have again and again experienced the blessings of our women teachers and prophets and healers. Our pastoral team includes six women proposed by the community as worthy of their confidence.

Thank God that throughout the Church the Spirit is not being quenched by the exclusion of women because of archaic social custom (the influence of the world).

FORMATION AND TRANSFORMATION

Borrowing the language of Rosemary Haughton from *The Transformation of Man*, we must see the Church as a community of people whose life, structure, and language can bring people from an initial encounter with Jesus to full maturity in the Body. The process of teaching and growing is both formation and transformation. The formative elements in the Church are continuous with the formative elements in the secular world: language, law, custom, guidance. This dimension of our life together takes into account all those elements in us that are not yet subject to the Spirit and so are still in need of the Law. We are free in Christ, of course, but not totally free until we are totally under the influence of the Spirit. From another point of view, our everyday life is more or less governed by custom, and this is the domain of formation.

Transformation occurs in all those choices which let love and the Spirit break through. In the concrete, in your life and mine, that happens because someone or a group challenges us to look beyond convention, beyond the superficial. Someone or a group calls forth the best in us, makes Jesus and His Spirit alive for us. Then the commonplace becomes illuminated with life, and life is transformed.

Now, let us be realistic. We are not with the Lord all day long. We lapse into ourselves and ordinary life constantly. But, what brings us forward is our time of prayer and our time with brothers and sisters who challenge us to let the Spirit break through.

The Church provides the setting for both formation and transformation. By saying that we should attend weekly meetings of the community at Sunday Mass, the Church is performing a formation function. She is saying: Come. Hear the Word. Share the Covenant Meal. Experience your brothers and sisters. Sometimes we do not feel like it (the priest does not either, sometimes), but we go anyhow. If we go with some faith that the *Lord* will do something, then something can happen. Within formative situations, transformation can occur—if we are open.

The Church is structured, with offices and services, because our humanity demands that. That is the formation, the secular part of life. But the Church, the life we have with our brothers and sisters in Jesus, offers us the constant challenge to be transformed by Christ's love. How loving God is to offer us a new life!

LEADERSHIP

All of this is possible only through the leadership which Jesus wants to provide, and "leadership" seems to be the right word for those holding office in the Body of Christ. To some extent, of course, we all exercise leadership in the Body, just as we all exercise the priesthood, but here my concern is the leadership of offices of the community.

In almost every case, the quality of community life in Christ depends on the quality of leadership. Whether official or unofficial, leadership is a determining factor. That is the way it is.

"Leadership" is a good word for those holding office in the Christian community. It reminds us all that we are dealing with a different kind of community and a different set of relations than worldly models. I believe that the following qualities are essential for the Christian leader to grow into.

1. Total honesty with himself/herself and others. Jesus calls us to live in the truth. A leader cannot call others to the truth unless he lives in it himself.

2. Total Commitment.

   (a) To seek the truth by continual study and prayer and spiritual direction. St. Francis de Sales said that learning is the eighth sacrament for a priest, so important is it. More harm is done by uninformed leaders than we can imagine. We need to know how to interpret God's Word, how to lead people to a deeper prayer life, how to help people learn to love. Some people would like to make prayer and the Bible their only source of learning, but the truth is that the folly of that is in evidence all around us. It has only been through the scholarship, the hard work of study, that we even have translations of the Bible available to us. One of the gifts the Lord gives us for building up the Body is intelligence. To bury that talent or to be negative about it is offensive to the Lord. There is nothing very good in being wrong about God. We also need to pray because the Lord wants to teach us a lot Himself. As we let the Spirit guide us in prayer, He brings to our minds the things He knows we need. And spiritual direction is a great instrument for learning as we engage in honest sharing of ourselves and our problems.

   (b) To a life of prayer. The Apostles knew well that their task was to pray in the service of the Word. We simply cannot be growing into the Lord unless we spend time alone with Him. A leader who does not pray lacks power.

   (c) To service. The leader is not to be served but to serve.

That is what he has authority for. He has to resist the special treatment that some would like to give him and, instead, give special treatment to others.

(d) To the full Gospel. The leader has to be uncompromising about the challenge of the whole Gospel first in his own life and secondly in his proclaiming of it. He cannot hesitate to speak the whole truth of Jesus. The Lord is preparing people's hearts to hear it, and how shall they believe unless the Word is preached.

(e) To seek the freedom of Christ. We are all so comfortable in our ruts, and in our bondage. Jesus calls us to freedom and this means breaking out of old patterns in order to live the freedom that will set others free. We discussed this in Volume III of this series. A leader must be free to sing, to rejoice, to love, to suffer, to speak the truth in love.

3. A leader must have the faith which claims God's promises. His faith must be the support of the faith of his brothers and sisters. I have often thought that the division of ministries by titles such as healing, pastor, prophet, etc., is misleading in the sense that some people think they should expect the Spirit to work in only one way in their lives. That is not the way it was with the Apostles and the saints. That is not the way it is with the people in our community. We seem to be used for whatever the needs are at the time: healing, prophecy, inspired teaching, etc. A leader must have the faith to claim God's power in the Spirit for all of God's promises.

4. A leader must share his life with others and be intimate with some. The call of Jesus is to become one with one another. Unless a leader actually shares himself with others, he will not know the crucifixion of love and its resurrection. His life and his message will lack the authority of the truth in his life.

5. A leader must have the ability and the desire to encourage, discover, and develop the talents and services of others. This means that the tone of his community will be set by an interest in persons rather than in structures, and, by the very fact of that love, makes it possible for structures to be adaptable and to be at

the service of persons. Discovering and developing talents and services depends both on personal interest and a whole atmosphere created by a loving community which is accepting, encouraging and positive. Leadership functions by encouraging all this and by seeing to it that the structures of the community life are involving rather than excluding. A long time ago I read somewhere that the best thing we can do for others is not to give them our best, but rather to help them discover their own.

6. A leader must never compromise the authority of the Gospel which is the call of the truth to full personal responsibility. One of the most common temptations of leaders is to be protective, maternal or paternal. Jesus preached the truth and allowed people to respond in their own way. Paternalism/maternalism does not trust personal freedom. It erects structures of accountability and supervision—and quenches the Spirit.

On the other hand, being uncompromising about personal responsibility involves the risk of many mistakes and a lot of frustration. It also offers the only sure road to solid growth. It is not neat and tidy and orderly, it does not achieve uniformity, but it is the way of the Gospel.

A community based on personal responsibility will treasure uniqueness of persons and life styles. Strong characters will abound. Praise God!

7. A leader must have a breadth of vision and involvement in life. It is the lived quality of the fullness of Christ's vision of all the world that stretches others, calls them forth to abundant life. Too many Christian communities have become one-dimensionally religious, missing the full glory of man and of the world, as well as the desperate need to serve the poor.

8. A leader must have a deep knowledge of history. So many mistakes that are made today have been made before and could be avoided. God speaks to us through history. Ignoring history is to ignore God's voice.

9. A leader must exhibit the fruits of the Spirit, the fruits of a deep relationship with Jesus and the Father and our brothers and sisters. "By their fruits you shall know them." Nothing more need be said.

10. A leader must be childlike, full of wonder, not taking himself too seriously.

CONCLUSION

If all we have said so far is taken seriously and lived, then a Christian community will evolve in which authority is not a problem. It will be a community of brothers and sisters who love each other and serve each other. Power relationships and power blocs are eliminated by all seeking the Lord's will together. People holding positions of responsibility will be brothers and sisters supported by other brothers and sisters in love. The structures will be the servants of persons and will maximize freedom. Behold a new thing: The Body of Christ.

BIBLIOGRAPHY

RECOMMENDED READING:

"Dogmatic Constitution on the Church." *The Documents of Vatican II.*
A document to be read carefully and prayerfully. A work of the Spirit.

McKenzie, John L., *Authority in the Church*, Sheed and Ward, New York, New York, 1966, 184 pp.
An absolute must for anyone who wants to understand the Christian (biblical) concept of authority. McKenzie is a special kind of Scripture scholar, simple, clear, and direct, with an international reputation for solid scholarship.

McGrath, O.P., Sister Albertus Magnus, *What a Modern Catholic Believes About Women*, Thomas More Press, Chicago, 1972, 127 pp.
Sister Albertus Magnus has a Ph.D. in history and has done a well documented study, yet easily readable, on the role of women in the Church and in Christianity. You cannot make up your mind about women's rights until you have read this book.

See also the other recommended readings about women in the lists at the end of Chapter 3.

by Anthony Cushing

States in Life 3

(Being Single, Marriage, Celibacy)

In this chapter we want to describe the ways we've seen God set us free in the different life-options we've chosen. We also hope to share what problems we've encountered and how we've worked out some of them. Since these areas are basic to all of us, we constantly need to explore and develop the ways in which God can transform our vocations. This is especially true in our present culture where we are being presented with a variety of questions, doubts, and solutions to how people should choose and live their state in life.

Because the topics are so broad, we cannot cover them with the thoroughness that some would like. The most we can do is to try to present a general overview on each topic. Also, we will deliberately avoid the complexities of moral codes and questions of domestic strategy. Father Lange will write the section on celibacy for obvious reasons.

ON BEING SINGLE

I am beginning with the single life because understanding of how the Lord works in the single life lays the groundwork for both Christian marriage and celibacy. Usually the single life is sort of brushed over because it's understood as temporary. You get the impression that people aren't to be taken seriously until they've made a life-commitment to marriage or celibacy. And there is a lot of truth to this because the normal social pattern is that the single life is an uncommitted life. However, for a Christian the single life is a life of radical commitment to Jesus and to Christian community. Therefore, we need to reverse our perspective. Instead of looking at the single life only as preparing for commitment, we need to look at being single as a way of commitment to the Lord.

SECURITY IN THE LORD

The basic direction of the single life is to establish a deep relationship with Jesus in community. All Christians (married, single, or celibate) are called to "love the Lord your God with all your heart, all your soul, all your mind, and with all your strength" and to "love your neighbor as yourself" (Mark 12:29). When a single person is totally dependent on God he finds his security and personal worth in simply being loved by God.

This runs directly contrary to the social expectations for single persons. We are conditioned to think that fulfillment and happiness can only be found in a sexual relationship. There is the great American romantic myth of total togetherness. "If only I find the right man (woman) then I will be really happy." Time and time again we've had people come into the community looking for a husband or wife. They experience this tremendous need for a sexual relationship and tend to latch on to the first person who shows any interest. Invariably these relationships end up neurotically and mutually destructive. These people are drawn together by their hunger for a perfect lover, someone who will totally accept them for what they are. Therefore, their relationship is based on need, on what is missing, not on the strength of the love they share. Having been in a few of these relationships myself, I know how much they feel like real love. And there is a tremendously powerful attraction. But it is the attraction of two vacuums drawn together and united by their emptiness.

What we have found is that people need to develop love relationships out of their strengths, not their weaknesses. Of course we all need someone to love us totally for what we are. For Christians this perfect lover is Jesus. He is the only one who can fulfill all their needs. When people experience this love as the basic reality of their lives, they are ready then for marriage or celibacy. As one girl put it, "I used to spend most of my time worrying when I'd be getting married. Then it finally dawned on me that I could be happy in Jesus whether I was married or not."

Over and over again we found that single people started to

have real peace about themselves when they gave up hunting for a mate. One by one the single people in our community reached the point of saying, "Lord, whatever you want for me will make me happy." After reaching this point of renunciation, they could relax and really start to enjoy life. The pressure was off; they could start to be themselves. Ironically enough, it was after this renunciation of seeking a mate that many people finally found one. Again, the big point is not seeking a relationship but seeking God's will first, whatever that might be.

COMMITMENT

All the Christian life-options are lives of commitment. In marriage and celibacy the life-option is based upon a primary commitment to God before the particular vocation is chosen. The single life is most often the time when people should be learning what it is to be a committed Christian.

Non-commitment is probably an epidemic among today's young adults. More and more people put off the decision for marriage or career and prefer to shop around. I, too, felt this inability to make a commitment. I think it's primarily a failure to find an ultimate meaning in life. Why commit yourself to marriage or career when you see all around you these commitments destroying people? It's another facet of the whole revolution of contemporary values. It ends up finding nothing that is ultimately valuable; therefore, my life has no direction; it's absurd.

Since these formative values of discipline, commitment, and dedication are losing impact on our contemporary culture, many Christians have to learn how to be committed to someone. This isn't so much a religious problem as a problem of never having worked out a life commitment before. People want to lead committed lives, but they simply don't know how.

For myself, it was only after working at my relationship with Jesus for a couple years that I started to understand what commitment meant. I learned the value of regular, open communication through my daily prayer life. As I experienced the deserts, I discovered the need to simply hang in there when I wasn't feeling God's love. This commitment set me free from my temporary moods and feelings. I was amazed that I could persevere in prayer and service when I really didn't feel like it. This helped me to overcome many fears about my own lack of faithfulness.

Only after experiencing the reality of my faithfulness with Jesus did I feel capable of making a commitment to marriage or celibacy. I knew that my basic direction in life was settled. I was going to follow Jesus. Since He was to be my basic security and strength, I could trust Him to help me work out whatever life-option I chose.

COMMUNITY

The literal idea of a *single* life is not what Christianity is about. Christians live a single life in community. This is where they learn what it means to love as Jesus did. As one newlywed put it:

> The community context I had chosen to live in made the major difference in my single life. No longer was I waiting to be committed to someone. I was already fully committed to a group of people. In community you accept the call to unconditional love and attempt to work through the intricacies of personal relationships. There are no retreats from this call to love. In the past it was my pattern to pack up and leave when things got too rough. Now I know I can work through any problems in relationships because that's what God helped me to do through my relationship in the community.

Learning to love the people in a Christian community is a real preparation for learning to love a spouse. There are people in community whom we really enjoy. It's easy to share ourselves with them in a friendship. There are also many people with whom we have very little in common. So we tend to remain on a superficial, acquaintance type relationship with them. And finally there are those we actually dislike, whom we have to struggle to understand and accept. These different kinds of relationships in a community are a mirror image of the different levels of a marriage relationship. There is a great deal that you should enjoy in your spouse, and that's easy to love. Also, there are areas of our lives that we do not share and there are things we dislike in our spouse. In all these areas of life together we need to learn how to love and be open to the power of the Spirit. Community, in this sense, is a kind of testing ground for our ability to love unconditionally in marriage. Obviously this also applies to celibacy, especially in the non-sexual characteristics of these relationships, since the celibate life is geared to loving service in community.

This testing ground for love is intensified in long-term friendships with both sexes and in Christian living situations or households. In both cases we are challenged to break out of our selfishness and isolation to learn how to love. In a household we are further confronted with the practicalities of working out a Christian life style together. Old habits taken for granted and patterns of behavior are revealed in the glaring light of honest love. Our moodiness, non-communication, and irresponsibility are broken by the simple fact of having to live together. Sharing a common life style helps us change the many little things that arguments are made of (like personal habits, chores, finances). For the last four years, I've lived in a Christian household. A lot of times it was fun and exciting, but it was also laden with conflicts and frustrations. I found that outside the house, I'm usually easy to get along with, but that my sloppiness and moodiness and forgetfulness make me less than an ideal roommate. The point is that this kind of community life reveals my probable strengths and weaknesses in terms of the practicalities of marriage. If I find it difficult to adjust my life style to a community, I might also find it difficult adjusting to my spouse.

Community also supports the single person through the wisdom of its experience. This is not only teaching, but the lived experience of "I've been through it before." This especially happens through married couples sharing their lives with single friends. For example, throughout the period of my engagement, a few married couples have regularly spent time talking and praying with my fiancée and me. They have helped us overcome a great many fears and misconceptions that we had about marriage. They have supported us in the rough times, prayed for us, and opened their homes and hearts to us so that we could grow in our relationship. Most of all, they have witnessed to us of the love and joy of Christian marriage so that we could have hope for our own marriage.

BUILDING RELATIONSHIPS

All of this brings us to the point of examining dating patterns for Christian singles. This is especially important since the contemporary models for dating and courtship are so inadequate. What we see most is a style of relationship geared toward well-intentioned deception to win a mate. The very structure of "getting dressed up for dinner and a show" often keeps a couple from experiencing each other in normal life situations. Going out on a date isn't wrong, but if that's all you do, chances are that it'll be difficult to really get to know each other.

Another destructive element of this kind of dating is that the male usually has the initiative. This means that a woman must please the man to continue being asked out. Without the initiative to continue a relationship, a woman can't be herself but constantly has to bargain for acceptance. This also leads women to compete with each other for a man's affection. The result is that many women find it difficult to have women-friends. Also, this puts women in the status of a sex object where she bargains her favors for the man's continued response.

Much of this is eliminated if it becomes a practice in a community for women to ask men for a date (and vice versa). In our group, we even recommended that women start to pay for some of the dates, and were roundly booed (by women) for that gem of liberation (the men cheered).

The basic way we've seen healthy romantic relationships develop is through Christian friendships. Community is a good place for men and women to get to know each other in non-threatening ways. There are group activities and simple non-romantic ways to get to know each other without the pressures of dating and sexual involvement. Friendship happens as people discover that they see the same things in life and enjoy the same activities. Romantic love is focused on the other person; friendship is two people focusing on something they share together. Developing friendships slows down the urgency of romantic relationships. People get a chance to decide if they want to develop a romantic relationship on the basis of first becoming friends. Otherwise relationships become too intense too soon and breaking them off becomes very painful, if not impossible. Developing friendships gives a couple a chance to have a more balanced perspective on their relationship. It becomes possible to relax in the love of God, enjoy themselves, and develop their talents; then their friendships will happen as a matter of course.

When a couple starts a romantic relationship it is important that they understand their relationship as Christ-centered. Each person should feel very strong in Jesus as the primary source of their security. For Christian couples, dating is a way of discovering God's will. This kind of love leaves the other person free to follow God's will whatever that might be. Until a public engagement, this relationship is clearly open-ended, unconditional, and non-possessive. In a sense each person must give up and renounce the other before marriage. They must die to each other in order for the relationship to come alive in Jesus.

Being non-possessive is the most difficult part of a relationship for me. There is the constant temptation to want to become my partner's savior and security. Over and over I have to realize that there are some ways that I cannot help the woman I love. Her fundamental needs must be met by Jesus. So I have to learn to direct her to Jesus for what I cannot give. Otherwise I am burdened with a perfection I cannot in any way live up to. She gets insecure because deep down she knows that I will eventually fail to love her. Thankfully the misery of this in both of us usually leads us to prayer and repentance.

Just as damaging is to expect another human being to be my savior. You start to demand love and affection as a kind of inalienable right. Because of this pressure, the other person literally cannot be himself or herself. They always have to be good because your need for love won't let them be weak.

However, if both partners experience the security of God's love through prayer, then they can love each other freely without bargaining for each other's affection. The basis of their relationship becomes *agape* love which is not connected at all with the beloved's goodness. This is to say, "I love you because I am a lover just as Jesus is a lover." This love endures even when the beloved fails to fulfill our expectations. This kind of love is forgiving no matter what. Often if our worth and security is primarily caught up in our partner's love, then we will probably find it excruciating if not impossible to forgive his or her wrongdoings. At times when I've experienced this inability to forgive, it has been just that my worth as a person was rooted first in my partner's love rather than Jesus. If my partner fails to love me, I feel I cannot forgive because I so much *need* someone to love me. I cannot forgive, because to forgive is to accept the fact that my partner does not love me all the time. If, however, my security is first of all in Jesus' love, I can forgive because I know that even though my beloved fails me, I am still accepted by Jesus.

This kind of love and forgiveness is the basis for the possibility of a life-long commitment to another person. This commitment becomes realistic because we have already experienced loving each other through thick and thin. This power to love is reliable, not because of our own abilities, but because it is the power of the Holy Spirit. "Let us love one another, because love comes from God" (1 John 4:7).

I said in the beginning that this would not be a discussion on moral codes. The Catholic teaching is that virginal chastity is the ideal for all single people. All the complexities and qualifications have been presented in many books. Among them are, "*Do you love me?*"

In terms of being responsible in expressing our sexuality, there are a number of helpful hints. First of all, if a couple is praying together regularly they can expect that the power of the Spirit will help them in expressing their sexuality with love and responsibility. Along with this, both partners need to be absolutely honest with their spiritual director about the degree of their sexual involvement. Communicating honestly with each other about sexual needs and expectations also helps us to learn responsibility to each other.

As a couple grows in commitment to each other and becomes engaged it makes sense that their expression of affection should grow also. One couple described this:

As our love and prayer for each other grew, it seemed that our sexual personalities were reborn. We were healed of the wounds and guilt of our past sexual relationships. There was a very natural balance in growth of our sexual expression along with our emotional, psychological, and spiritual growth together. It was almost as if God were purifying us and preparing us to be virginal and innocent for our wedding.

PRAYER, DISCERNMENT AND HEALING

The basic criteria for discerning marriage is the quality of the relationship itself. Are the two people really loving one another freely and bringing each other closer to God? Is their friendship bringing each other to maturity? Do they communicate well and together work through problems? This is simply to see beginning in their relationship the elements of a good Christian marriage. After all, deciding to marry is not just a momentary inspiration that you experiment with to see if it's from the Lord. Nor can you wait till after marriage to check for the fruits of this charism as you would with a ministry. So, in some way, you have to be able to discern the effects of this relationship before marriage.

Along with this is each person's prayer experience of God's approval of the relationship. It's also a good idea to test this discernment with spiritual directors and other mature Christians. I know it was a real help in our engagement to hear that other people saw the way we were growing because of our relationship. This was especially true when the parish pastor with all his experience of the problems of marriage predicted an enviable marriage for us. More importantly, he said this after helping us resolve a problem that we had found impossible to solve by ourselves.

Discernment is made easier when a Christian couple actually experiences being healed and set free by each other's love. During our engagement we both were dramatically changed through each other's love. We saw whole new areas of our personality develop as we learned to love each other without conditions. Of course, there are times in the dynamic of any relationship when one or the other becomes selfish or possessive. But this just opens the door for the healing of our old wounds and hurts. This happened most clearly once when we were praying about my fear of getting married. Through this prayer I began to see that this was a basic fear in me of being held down or limited in any way. As a result I was fiercely independent and resistant to any signs of weakness or dependence on another person. Part of my being healed of this was experiencing Jesus' love in those areas of my past when I had felt tied down or limited (little things like being physically held down, almost suffocating once in the first grade, being unjustly punished by teachers, etc.). However, the more thorough healing came about as I learned to depend on my fiancée to love me in my weakness.

Now I am awed at the joy and beauty that this woman has brought into my life. In her love, I see the wildness, passion, and tenderness of Jesus' love for me. I feel free and whole as I've never felt before. This love, more than anything else, has helped Jesus re-create me to begin to taste of the "freedom of the sons of God" (Romans 8).

CONCLUSION: A WORD ON ROMANCE

After saying all of this I would like to rejoice in the fact that even charismatic Christians are human. We have all made many mistakes and will probably continue to do so in the future. And, good advice notwithstanding, people in love will probably continue to do the same silly things they've been doing since time began. And even though people get hurt, we must avoid taking our Christian clichés too seriously.

Personally I think that when it comes to the problems of dating and sexuality, many Christian writers seem to have forgotten the mistakes of their youth. Unfortunately it is far too easy to forget the passions of our own heart and expect others to live up to something we might have found impossible to do. It's easy to get the impression that these people would try to guard us from the very mistakes they themselves made. As good intentioned as this is, it usually doesn't work. Romance is remarkably immune to common sense. Falling in love is a kind of temporary insanity where we all expect people to be slightly foolish. If such lovers were to become prudent, we would all be missing something very beautiful and wild. We cannot so concentrate on the dangers and evils of romance that we smother its God-given goodness. One is reminded of Jesus' parable to be wary of rooting out the weeds lest we pull up the wheat along with it.

You see, I have made my share of mistakes in romance, spectacular mistakes that have caused great harm and led me to the brinks of insanity. Yet I wouldn't have missed it for all the world. As painful as they were, these failures are precious to me. There was great joy as well as agony. I learned to love through those women, and without them I would be impoverished. I believe that they were God's way of making me real. And the extravagance of these failures in love in some way revealed to me the extravagance and wildness of Jesus' love for his people, his bride, the Church.

So my mistakes are too numerous and too recent for me to forget easily. And I don't want to forget them. As a result I cannot prescribe any set formula. Perhaps it's the realization that the people who would most need that good advice would be the ones least likely to listen to it. Perhaps good advice on romance is only for us to say, "Yes, I should have done it that way." And perhaps that's good.

All I can say is love, pray, get a good spiritual director and try not to take yourself too seriously. But then lovers always take themselves too seriously.

CHRISTIAN MARRIAGE

Love, which was always held up to us as the answer to life's predicaments . . . has now become the problem (Rollo May, as quoted in E. Schillebeeckx, *Marriage: Human Mystery and Saving Reality*, p. 40).

Love is the problem. "Whom do I love? How do I love? How long do I love?" The love problem is epidemic in our present society. Love and marriage seemingly go together rarely. People are forsaking and mocking what their parents considered sacred. At no other time has there been so much known and written about how people live their marriages. Alongside this knowledge is the chronic failure to live out their marriages successfully. As Carl Rogers has noted in his book *Becoming Partners*, when more than 50% of the marriages end up in divorce (as in California), perhaps we had better look for alternatives. And plenty of alternatives have been presented, ranging from communal marriages to old-fashioned "shacking-up." Whatever the causes of this situation, it's at least an exciting (and humorous) time to live.

We see and hear around us new questions and new answers about marriage. Some of these are good and loving; others are rubbish. This is bound to happen any time the traditions and customs of a society break down. One thing, however, is certain, we cannot demand that that past come back to life. As Christians we need to deal with the present realities and discover how God can help us develop Christian marriages in this present society.

One more caution before we begin. All of us are experts on marriage. We watched our parents' marriage, maybe lived our own or helped and hindered our friends in their marriages. Because of this familiarity we have a tendency to think that the way we've seen and lived marriage is *the right way* to be married. All of us (of course, myself included) have the particular blinders of our environment. My Polish background led me to believe that a passion for Kielbasa (a Polish sausage) was part of human nature. For Christians these blinders also include some favorite teaching which might be out of perspective (as indeed this teaching might be). So if you feel yourself reacting negatively to something I say, take a minute to pray and reflect on where this reaction comes from (parents, friends, old habits, teachers), and then decide which you choose to believe. Consider this a process of dialogue with the book, an open-ended seeking of the truth.

"MARRIAGE IN THE LORD" (1 CORINTHIANS 7:34)

For this reason a man shall leave his father and mother and shall cling to his wife, and the two shall be made into one. Thus they are no longer two but one flesh. Therefore, let no man separate what God has joined (Matthew 19:5-6).

Husbands, love your wives, as Christ loved the Church. He gave himself up for her to make her holy (Ephesians 5:25).

A wife does not belong to herself but to her husband; equally a husband does not belong to himself but to his wife (1 Corinthians 7:4).

His disciples said to him, "If that is the case between man and wife, it is better not to marry." He (Jesus) said, "Not everyone can accept this teaching, only those to whom it is given to do so . . . Let him accept this teaching who can" (Matthew 19:10, 12).

The glory of Christian marriage is that it is a challenge to total love and faithfulness. As the disciples knew, this was impossible for sinful and selfish mankind. Jesus did not simply lay down a law but he gave us the power to live in a new way. He gave us the Spirit that we might love as He loved. The depth of this love is so awesome that it is foolishness for the world. In Jesus, ordinary marriage is caught up in this mystery of God's love and made holy. It becomes something bigger than friendship, desire, convenience, and comfort. This "foolishness" of God's love is to make marriage a sacrament, a sign of His presence in the world. The love, forgiveness and faithfulness of two people in marriage is to be the symbol of the God who is love, who is a community of persons united in love.

When Paul talks about the kind of love married partners are to have for each other, he compares this to the way Christ loves His Church. "This is a great foreshadowing (mystery); I mean that it refers to Christ and the Church." (Eph. 5:32) That marriage is a mystery refers to two things:

1. Mystery (Latin sacramentum) is the way in which God acts for man in history.

2. Mystery is something that cannot be completely grasped with our minds. As Gabriel Marcel said, mystery is "infinitely discoverable." God is mystery. We are each a mystery. We can know God and each other only partially, there is always more. We can always be surprised.

Jonathan Hanaghan, Christian psychologist and poet, at the age of 72 still has the hope to write of this mystery:

Until man and woman have carried their confrontation to the point where they discover the real essence of each other, they have not learned the meaning of the sex relationship; they have not come face to face with the mystery of it all. Until they reach the point where . . . they are filled with

wonder, they have not discovered the real beauty of a fulfilled sexual relationship.

Youth is now exploring this intangible world of spiritual
loveliness where a man does not know his manhood until it is
mirrored and present in womanhood, and a woman does not
know her womanhood until it is presented in the spirituality
of a man who loves her . . .

The poets, especially the English poets, have always
sensed the beauty and graciousness of the true sexual life.
Spencer gives us the vision of a boy looking into a girl's eyes,
seeing the beauty that is in her soul, and she can't see it, but
through his words and his glances, she awakes to him and
her soul is born into immortal beauty. She responds to him
and is literally made, recreated by his love, *for the lover literally creates his beloved*; she becomes something that she
never imagined she could be (*The Courage To Be Married*,
Jonathan Hanaghan, Abbey Press, St. Meinrad, Indiana,
1974, p. 2).

The mystery is that love lets us become who we really are.
Christ loves the Church and gives His life to "make her holy."
He sees in us a beauty that we cannot believe. His love transforms
us to the point where we start to see ourselves the way He sees us
—we are beloved. The joy of the beloved is to see herself through
the eyes of her lover. This is the joy of Christianity and the mystery of marriage. I discover who I am because I find myself in
your love for me.

Perhaps we need a poetry of marriage as well as theology.
All love is a mystery and paradox, both with the Lord and in
marriage where we cry out,

Take me to you, imprison me, for I never shall be free,
Except you enthrall me,
Nor even chaste, except you ravish me.

(Holy Sonnet 14, John Donne,
Norton Anthology of English Literature)

Married Christians are to give their lives to each other in
such a total way as to make each other holy, to make them truly

themselves as God sees them. Marriage as a sacrament and a charism (1 Corinthians 7) is not only to reflect this love of Christ but to give married people the power to love each other in this kind of way. That this sacrament "effects what it signifies" is simply to say that if people seek God and His power in their marriage, God will give them the help they need to live that marriage.

Vatican II summarizes this whole idea of marriage as a sacrament of love and faithfulness to make us holy:

Thus a man and a woman, who by the marriage covenant of conjugal love "are no longer two, but one flesh" (Matt. 19:6), render mutual help and service to each other through an intimate union of their persons and of their actions. Through this union they experience the meaning of their oneness and attain to it with growing perfection day by day. As a mutual gift of two persons, this intimate union, as well as the good of the children, imposes total fidelity on the spouses and argues for an unbreakable oneness between them.

Christ the Lord abundantly blessed this many-faceted love, welling up as it does from the fountain of divine love and structured as it is on the model of His union with the Church. For as God of old made Himself present to His people through a covenant of love and fidelity, so now the Savior of men and the Spouse of the Church comes into the lives of married Christians through the sacrament of matrimony. He abides with them thereafter so that, just as He loved the Church and handed Himself over on her behalf, the spouses may love each other with perpetual fidelity through mutual self-bestowal.

Authentic married love is caught up into divine love and is governed and enriched by Christ's redeeming power and the saving activity of the Church . . .

By virtue of this sacrament as spouses fulfill their conjugal and family obligations they are penetrated with the Spirit of Christ. This Spirit suffuses their whole lives with faith, hope and charity. Thus they increasingly advance their own perfection as well as their mutual sanctification, and hence contribute jointly to the glory of God (*Constitution on the Church in the Modern World*, n. 48).

Over the last 4½ years, our community life has led us to a rather obvious discovery: Christian marriage is supposed to be lived through the power of the Holy Spirit. To attempt to live this kind of life-style I described before, without experiencing the help of God, is foolish and frustrating. The Church has recognized this in that a marriage between unbaptized persons is not held as binding as a Christian marriage is. In our society we see the disastrous results of people attempting to live a Christian marriage without the help of God.

Edward Schillebeeckx in his book *Marriage: Human Reality and Saving Mystery* notes that in the past the very structure of society helped preserve marriage. The stability of the marriage was external to the couple. The economics, politics, and customs of previous societies kept marriages together. Today, however, this external security is not to be taken for granted, but it is something to be achieved by the couple themselves. In other words, there is less social pressure keeping a couple together. Because of this, Christian couples are almost forced to depend more on the Lord for the power to live their marriages.

Most of what we've learned about living a Christian single life is the basis for Christian marriage. In a Christian marriage each person has to find his or her ultimate security in the Lord. Together they must learn to "seek first the Kingdom." The root of their relationship should be agape love, to love each other as brother and sister in the Lord as well as lover, friend, and partner. It is this intense fullness of love which is the concrete witness of the immensity of Jesus' love for His Church. When a couple has this kind of powerful non-possessive love they are, in a real sense, saving and healing each other.

This healing is not just through joy of loving but also through the endurance of loving. Christian marriage exists to root out the selfishness in each other. In this total nakedness, of which intercourse is only the symbol, Christian spouses are to love and accept each other. Especially when all that the world says is, "Leave, save yourself," Christian love witnesses the tenderness and patience that Jesus has with us. And the only reason we can do this is because God gives us the power to love like His Son.

This is what Hanaghan calls "prayerful non-recrimination."

A husband does not know how to love his wife until he encounters the bitch in her, is the object of abuse, and lets her release her frustration and anger on him (and vice-versa).

And this is the cross of Christian marriage, to accept her and not to abandon her. And so the true man and true woman *burn* into each other (*The Courage To Be Married, op. cit.,* p. 29).

The source of this kind of healing love is in prayer, community, and the sacraments. For a Christian marriage these things must become practical priorities. If a couple understands their marriage as dependent on the power of God, then a big part of their relationship is to build up each other's faith. This entails witnessing to each other, studying and encouraging each other in community involvements. All of this is done with the attitude that "one of the best ways I can love you is to help you get closer to Jesus." I can't help thinking of a couple in our community who 15 years ago thought it important to go to Mass together every day during their engagement to see if God wanted them together. However, once married, the everyday routines of marriage so overwhelmed them that this was no longer important. After that they gradually lost touch with their marriage as a sacrament in the Lord. Only after becoming involved in the community did they relearn this wisdom of their engagement.

I suppose the hardest part of building each other's faith is finding time together to pray. Most couples need to structure a set time and place into their weekly routine, otherwise the hectic pace of family life tends to absorb a couple's prayer time.

Very often married couples who met the Lord after they were married find it almost embarrassing to pray together. What happens is that a couple has gotten to know each other in a certain way, and praying or witnessing just doesn't fit into our picture of who that person is. As a result it seems artificial and phony. Most of the time, perseverance and a sense of humor take care of this problem.

A big part of what happens in prayer would be a deeper self-revelation and prayer for inner healing. In all of us there are fears and patterns of behavior that we seem to have no control over.

71

There are arguments that have no mutually satisfying resolutions. In these situations we need to trust that God will heal those hurts which keep us from loving each other. (Cf. Vol. III.)

What we've seen happen to married couples in our community is something like a resurrection of a relationship. One couple confessed that they hadn't really communicated for over 15 years until they made a retreat together. After that they found a whole new kind of affection and tenderness for each other. The husband began to spend more time at home with the family and just wasting time with his wife. Another couple felt that their already good marriage became surprisingly better:

We had gotten so busy doing our daily routines that we had lost sight of the basics of our marriage vows. We no longer spent enough time building up our own relationship and our relationship with the children. When we came to know the Lord and opened our lives to His direction, the biggest result was that we opened up to each other. Knowing Jesus helped us to be more open and honest with each other, how we feel. We found that we were able to work through the things we didn't like about each other and to continue to love each other. We came to an agreement on our priorities so that first of all we spend more time learning how to love each other and the children.

WHAT KIND OF MARRIAGE?

In the history of the Church there have been many models and structures for marriage. In most of these models love was not seen as necessary for a marriage to survive. Paul's exhortation for the husband to "love his wife as his own body" was radically different than the expectation of the Roman culture. (Note: It was incomprehensible that the wife would love the husband so Paul only asks for respect and obedience.) Marriage was usually a social arrangement, and if love was there, all the better. However, now love is seen as the center of marriage. The expectations of contemporary marriage would seem silly to our grandparents. You can see this in one of the songs from "Fiddler on the Roof." Tevye after seeing his daughters fall in love asks his wife, "Do you love me?" She responds, "For 25 years I cooked your meals, washed your clothes, slept with you. Do I love you?" But that is not enough for him. He keeps on asking, "Do you love me?" as if to say "I know you do things for me, but do you love me?" And so, for all of us, love becomes the problem in marriage.

We found that love should be the description and language of marriage. You don't need to talk about social and sexual roles, you need to talk about love. Who has the authority is not the question. How we love is the only question. We don't need to impose any particular structure on marriage except that which helps two people love each other.

MUTUALITY

Where there is love there is no will to power (Carl Jung).

Submit yourselves to one another, because of your reverence for Christ (Ephesians 5:21—TEV).

A husband and wife are equal before the Lord and this loving equality is best described as a relationship of mutuality. One does not try to dominate the other but both are to "love each other with perpetual fidelity through mutual self-bestowal" (*Constitution on the Church in the Modern World*, n. 48).

This is clearly seen in receiving the sacrament of marriage. Marriage is not "administered" by the priest or by the husband. The essence and form of the sacrament is the couple's free choice of each other. If the sacrament begins in this free, mutual choice, then I would suppose that the action of the sacrament continues through that free choice. This means that one does not inflict his will on the other, but both spouses together choose to follow God. No one can command someone to marry. In the same way no spouse can command obedience from the other. To love as Christ loved is to love your spouse to transform him or her. This calls for patient acceptance and understanding of each other's weaknesses. This is how Christ loves the Church. He does not dominate us but He serves us. He does not coerce, but He loves us to the point where we are free to love. Two thousand years of imperfect sinful Christians is a marvelous witness to the acceptance and patience of Jesus. This is how we are to love each other in marriage.

DECISION MAKING

The big issue is not who's boss. The important issue is two people trying to love one another (a father in our community).

Because marriage is a sacrament in the loving choice of two people, you would hope that the decisions in that marriage continue to be the loving choice of two people. Again the question isn't one of authority or expertise but "*How do we, in love, discern the will of God for us?*"

The first decision for a couple is, "What kind of marriage are we going to have?" Neither the Church nor society can tell the couple how they are to relate to each other. This is the couple's own decision to make (within the limits of Church and state law).

As for styles of marriage and decision making in our community, people are trying out different things. A few of the couples have a kind of male leadership by mutual choice. Most of the couples have a structure of mutual decision making. Both of these styles have benefits and limitations. On a whole, all the couples tend toward mutuality even though they might not express it that way. For example, one married father of five expressed his leadership as: "Sure, I guess we usually follow my decisions. It's just because I've got a big mouth and my wife is more flexible than I am."

In a Christian marriage, decision making is discerning God's will. That means a couple needs to pray and talk together until they are of "one heart and mind" about a decision. This might seem to take a long time but in fact there aren't that many immediate decisions that need to be made in a marriage. If there is time to talk and pray about a situation then there is time to come to a mutual agreement on the most difficult topics. You only need a central authority in task-oriented situations where immediate decisions are needed. Another father who sees his role as leadership noted that in reflecting about it he can say that he and his wife always made decisions by mutual agreement. Especially in important decisions, there is always time to wait to be sure you're both hearing God's voice.

In regard to models of decision making we have to remember that we are talking about two people discerning God's will. This discernment has a different dynamic than decision making in large organizations. This was summarized by a retired navy captain speaking of his marriage of 25 years. "You don't run a marriage like a construction company. There's no boss. Sometimes I've got a good idea and we follow that. Other times my wife has the better idea and so we go that way."

Practically, this works out in terms of each partner's expertise in a given field. Sometimes one of the partners has little experience or knowledge in a certain area of life (i.e., medicine, finances, jobs, school) and so one relies on the spouse's experience to make the decision. This kind of respect for each other's judgment is not merely humble but it allows the best in each partner to be expressed.

COMMUNICATION

"You just have to keep on talking to each other no matter what."

When I first heard this, I thought it would be an easy thing to do. I mean, people in love just naturally want to share who they are with their beloved. As I learned more about people's everyday experience I started to see just how difficult this really is. Communication is the key to a healthy relationship. It is the quality of communication that governs the quality of the relationship.

Finding time for loving communication is fairly easy for most people who are dating. Most of the time they spend together is to get to know each other. After sharing their life and experiencing each other in their strength and weakness they can finally believe that they can trust each other's love. What is strange, though, is that many couples, after they are married, fail to take the time to share together. The business of everyday routines carries people along to the point where they wake up sleeping with a spouse who has become a stranger. All this because they failed to continue the sharing that made their relationship possible in the first place.

A couple needs to spend time together to share. This is the soul of the marriage—how they love when they are alone with their spouse. I know a couple for whom this is so important that for the last 42 years they have gone out to dinner twice a week just so they can have time to talk to each other.

Well, what do you talk about? As one woman friend once said, "As he can thrill me like no one else, he can bore me like no one else." It is the challenge of marriage to keep on communicating throughout a lifetime. Much more than finding the time to share, the challenge is to continue to risk sharing; to be vulnerable to the person who can hurt so much; to continue to share even when the other seems bored; to hang in there through weeks, months or years when the other is incapable of real communication. To risk discovering the other, to be willing to let him or her surprise me, to accept him or her changing and growing; this is the most awesome challenge and the only way to become really one.

Honest and open communication reveals both goodness and weakness. Most of the time people tend to emphasize the difficulty of sharing negative feelings, but positive feelings seem pretty difficult also. What we discover is that we need to be able to tell our beloved the treasure that he or she is. We need to learn how to praise and to let our beloved see the goodness that we see in him or her. This reminds me of the greatest double-ended compliment by the navy captain I mentioned earlier. His wife was moaning, "I'm just so stupid. I just never do anything right." He responded, "Honey, you couldn't be stupid, you married me." How often do you see married couples complimenting each other to their face? Somehow the impression is given that this only happens when you're dating. For example, two newlyweds can walk along holding hands and kissing and everyone thinks it's great. But, if that continues for 10 years, people think that it's odd that they haven't gotten over that yet. Society conditions us to expect that marriage will get stale and that you'll have to "simply put up with each other."

However, what we've seen is that the power of the Spirit is to lead couples to greater and greater intimacy. The Marriage Encounter program is just one of the ways the Spirit is working to renew Christian marriage. The effects of this program on good marriages is almost unbelievable. We see couples return all hugs and kisses, complimenting each other, sharing prayer together. And this lasts and grows as it overflows into daily life.

Jerry and Mary Mandry, members of the Board of Directors of Marriage Encounter, Inc., in their article entitled "Healing in Marriage" (*New Catholic World*, July-August 1975, pp. 178-179) write:

In the early years of our marriage, most of our time and energy was spent getting to know one another. Like any other happily married couple, we spent much of our time simply enjoying each other and what we were doing. This was always (and still is) relatively easy and natural, for we have much in common. We like a lot of the same things, have a similiar outlook on life and, best of all, have the same goals and hopes for the future. As time passed, we seemed to be more bound together because of all we had in common.

And so we thought that the more we shared together, the closer we would become. We were conscious of the need to work at our marriage and tried to do all we could to be a couple.

However, we began to sense that despite all our similarities and "togetherness" there had to be something more. We simply were not "one in mind, one in heart and one in affection." There was something missing—something that kept us from enjoying the total closeness or intimacy we longed for.

About this time we were awakened to the importance of sharing our feelings with one another. We learned that feelings are the most intimate and personal part of us. Yet it was the part to which we paid the least attention.

We were well tuned in to each other in what we liked or didn't like, and what we believed or questioned and why. We even expressed feelings, as long as they were acceptable or justifiable. Still much of each of us remained hidden from the other after all the years we lived as husband and wife.

This is the "more" that we were looking for—the need to share deep feelings that we had tried to bury or eliminate. We were middle-aged before we understood that there is no morality attached to feelings. How we act on our feelings determines the morality, but the feelings can't be right or wrong, good or bad. They are simply an important part of who we are.

Once we discovered this, we knew that there was a whole new world for us to explore together. We found new feelings we weren't even aware of in ourselves. These had to be shared, along with the rest of us, if we were to intimately experience each other.

It was amazing for us to discover that our relationship could be so much fuller, richer and deeper. In keeping parts of ourselves private, our motives were good. What was hidden was usually that part of "self" that we considered not quite good enough for the other. There were so many feelings that we could never reveal to anyone, so many fears and doubts that seemed to make us less than what we wanted to be. We didn't talk about our fear of dying, our shame in never adequately experiencing God, our feelings of indifference to those around us as well as toward each other, anxiety about money, resentment over jobs. These were the "unacceptable" kind of feelings that remained deep inside us. We wanted to show our "best" self rather than our "whole" self. It seemed more sensible to keep our relationship peaceful rather than rock the boat. It wasn't so much that we doubted the other's love, as much as we questioned our own lovableness.

Each new day gives us an exciting opportunity to experience our spouse's ever changing feelings. Sharing our deepest feelings of anxiety, pleasure, fear and joy enriches the "uniqueness" of our beloved. Today we are different people than we were yesterday. Our feelings change constantly, so if we are to become truly intimate we have to continue to try to experience the other's uniqueness on a daily basis.

If you're ever seen a couple after making the Marriage Encounter, you know what intimacy is—all because people learned communication and how to bring Jesus into their marriage. And the basic tool of Marriage Encounter is to simply write down what you feel about a particular aspect of your marriage and share it with your spouse. Admittedly, this is a bit artificial, but it's just to help people get to the point where they do it naturally. A big part of this sharing is about negative feelings that we were afraid to share. "I can't stand your cooking. Our sex life is a bore. I feel worthless, like a failure, ugly." There are good and bad ways to communicate these feelings. (Cf. Vol. III.) We had a mother in our community who, after 25 years of marriage found herself screaming to her husband, "I don't believe you love me anymore." She later admitted this was just a way of reminding him that he had stopped doing "all those nice things" for her. If both parties remember that feelings have no moral value, then they can learn to deal with them and to change their behavior accordingly. Absolute honesty about what I am feeling is usually healthy and it prevents those big blow-ups of repressed frustration. However, this needs to be balanced by love, sensitivity, and intelligence. A good caution is Keith Miller's story about the man who attended a Christian workshop on communication and then went home and opened up to his wife about an adulterous affair he had had. His wife ended up having a nervous breakdown. The relationship needs to have some stability in love before this kind of sharing can take place.

The end result of open communication is that a couple learns to appreciate the mystery of each other. They can be surprised by their lover because they have been willing to be themselves. Then two people enter into a contemplative union with each other. They can be silent or exuberant, and greatest of all is the deep peace and freedom of being loved. As Jonathan Hanaghan writes:

> We must struggle to find truth and light in our relationships as man and woman. A man and a woman know so little about each other even after they have slept with each other for years. Because I think that the end result of it all is mystery, instead of arriving at knowledge as you thought and as sex books will tell you, you discover the whole thing is a mystery. All of my life I have studied it and I am now 72 but

I have more sense of the mystery of life than I had when I was 20. As my experience grew my knowledge seemed to disappear. When a man and a woman get really close to one another, there is nothing to say, nothing to explain. . . . Harmony is resolution after conflict, a rest after strain, a solution after profound differences. . . . I am married and I feel free as the air. I am in love and I know that I am loved and I haven't got the slightest dread or fear (*The Courage To Be Married, op. cit.*, pp. 40-41).

CONFLICT

Someone once said that in marriage the two shall become one, and that the question is: Which one?

Because two people love and share their innermost selves with each other, conflicts are bound to arise. Once I feel loved enough to be myself, both the saint and the sinner is released in me. I just heard it tonight from a husband. "People think I'm the model of patience; only my wife knows what a grouch I really am." Marriage exposes our selfishness in order to heal it. Marriage has great power to heal and to hurt. Nowhere else are we as vulnerable. It's a dangerous and risky situation to try to love someone for life. There are all kinds of surprises—discoveries of love and of hate. I often think of marriage as a nuclear reactor, very helpful but very dangerous. Hanaghan describes it:

Marriage offers the jungle to live in to find the splendor of the Kingdom of Heaven. Marriage isn't worth a penny until one or the other partner has the courage to strike into the fundamental selfishness of the other and lay it bare, and fight the fight that is necessary to bring one's mate to reality (*The Courage To Be Married, op. cit.*, p. 49).

Jesus calls us to "die to ourselves" and marriage is the accelerated program in dying. We are literally forced from our self-centeredness. There is always someone else to consider. *My* desires have to be balanced by *our* desires. This intensity leads to the kind of conflict that can break down our false images of ourselves and release the power of the Spirit in our lives.

This release of power is to bring the peace of Jesus into our lives. This is peace not as the world gives it. It's not the peace of good order, politeness, or routine (though they are part of it). It's the peace of knowing I'm loved, knowing that we can work through the problems in the power of the Spirit. Most of the couples in our community witness about this peace that comes with the resolution of conflicts. It's the old cliché about "sure we fight, but it's great making up." It's no coincidence that many people experience their greatest moments of sexual union after resolving conflicts. Conflict makes us vulnerable. "Here's the stark naked me, love me or leave me." And when we're loved in that basic nakedness of self we can experience real intimacy. Ecstasy (to be out of myself) is possible because I no longer have to defend myself.

The reason I'm making such a big issue of this is that many people seem to think that love and conflict are incompatible. Part of the reason for this is that as children many of us never saw our parents resolving conflicts. Either they were hidden from the children or there was a tremendous outburst of anger and violence followed by a truce but not a resolution. Sometimes we have this idea that Christians should never argue but always be meek and mild. What we've experienced is that conflicts can expose our selfishness so that we can deal with it. I am no lover of argument but I realize that I can *learn to argue creatively.* Conflict is not the simple release of anger and frustration. It is to lead to a mutual decision to change.

There are some guidelines here. (Cf. *The Intimate Enemy: How To Fight Fair in Love and Marriage.*) Beware of "kitchen sink fights" where you bring up old wounds and scars. Try to stick to the present. Avoid "round robin" arguments where all you do is go over the same point time and again ("Yes, I did. No, you didn't"). Talk about what *you feel*, not what you think your partner is trying to do. Learn from the animals and have a "play dead" ritual which tells your partner to absolutely lay off because this hurts too much. Try to aim for a mutual decision, not a surrender to my way.

Conflicts don't have to be violent or terribly destructive. There are ways to learn how to handle conflicts that don't destroy. The emphasis here is on learning.

I don't mean to give the impression that a good Christian couple should be fighting all the time or even frequently. Our nerves just couldn't stand it. The point is to *learn how to resolve conflicts.* Most arguments seem to come from poor communication or a breakdown of communication. This means learning skills in how to talk to each other so that these unnecessary conflicts are avoided. Even if a couple is truly communicating who they are to each other some conflicts will result. However, they will probably not reach the kind of peak anger that so terrifies us. Basically, Christian couples can handle these conflicts of selfishness because they know that they have the power of the Spirit to love. Through prayer the hardest hearts can melt. As one man said, "When we find it impossible to live with each other, we can always turn to Jesus with the ultimate prayer, 'Help!' "

SETTING EACH OTHER FREE

Marriage is a way to become holy and free. Each of us has patterns of behavior and insecurities that need to be healed. Conflict exposes the sickness in all of us, and so Christian couples need to learn how to lead each other to God for healing. Here I want to focus on our unauthentic social and sexual role patterns.

Couples tend to start off living their parents' marriage. Usually they are the only model we have for *the right way* to be married. Keith Miller tells the story about how in his family his father never did any domestic chores. In his wife's family the father always took out the garbage. After their honeymoon his wife asked him to take out the garbage and he felt that his masculinity was insulted and angrily refused, leaving her sulking and confused. This is a little thing, but it causes big problems.

The larger areas entail "what a real wife (husband) is supposed to be." "Take charge," the man hears all his life. "Let her know who's boss." The woman learns "how to please her man," to be a fascinating female and a homebody. I don't know how much truth there is in these sexual roles. Obviously there are psychological as well as physical differences between men and women. However, we need to discover our own sexual role and identity, not just take for granted the clichés of our childhood.

Whatever we learned in the past, the fact is that a great many people are dissatisfied with the traditional sexual roles and are looking for new ways to express their sexual identity.

This is not an issue of condemning the past or plunging into the new wave of the future. It is an issue of discovering God's will for each person. I am a unique person and a great deal of my Christian liberation is discovering my sexual identity in Christ. What if the wife is better at organization and the husband delights in cooking? What about the times when father is weak and insecure and the mother the strength of the family? What if the wife is the breadwinner or more intelligent? How can I be myself along with fulfilling the sexual roles expected of me?

Basically we've seen that as people become more secure in love they can let go of unauthentic sexual and social roles. This applies to unauthentic "liberated" roles as well as the traditional ones. In one case a wife came to realize that she had kept her husband on a pedestal for twenty years. She felt spiritually inferior to him. He was always the strong one who made the decisions in the house. As a result he felt terribly burdened by this responsibility of being super-human and perfect. He literally couldn't be himself around his wife. He had to be strong for her. In turn she felt like a doormat because she always seemed stupid next to him. After they came into the community, the wife began to feel more and more worthwhile through the love of Jesus and the community. Gradually she began to see all kinds of talents and abilities in herself that she never could admit to before. As she started to assert her ideas in the marriage, problems developed. Her husband had quite a hard time dying to his old self-image of the boss of the family. Even though he really wanted to be free of this burden, he couldn't let go of his pattern of superiority. Gradually through a lot of pain he was capable of admitting his weakness and being vulnerable to his wife. This was such an identity crisis that for a while his wife had to be the strong one in the marriage. Now there's a balance and a mutuality where they support each other and can accept each other's strengths and weaknesses.

Just the opposite was the case in another marriage. The husband came from a family where the father refused to participate in making decisions and so the mother ended up running the home. (Sociologists say that this kind of American matriarchy is surprisingly widespread.) The result was a kind of fear of female domination.

This fear could have been heightened by his marriage to a very beautiful, intelligent, and extroverted woman. However, she chose to support him in a leadership role. What is especially important for both of them is that the wife is doing this in love for the husband. It's seen not just as a practical structure but as a way of loving and healing each other. This has gone a long way toward healing the husband of his fear of domination. And his wife is being set free from a pattern of excessive independence inherited from her response to an overly-strict upbringing. And the tenderness and joy of their love for one another is a genuinely exciting witness to the whole community.

A Christian couple is to be a source of grace for each other through their love. It is this unconditional love which lays bare the selfishness and phoniness that all of us have. And it is in this atmosphere of love and acceptance that psychological healing most readily takes place. Christian marriage roots out the seeds of our shallowness and unauthenticity. We are constantly challenged to grow, and growth is painful as well as exhilarating. But as a couple open themselves to the power of the Spirit this growth becomes more and more an everyday experience in their marriage. Old taken-for-granted roles and patterns are broken down because we more and more experience being loved for who we are. And this security of being loved literally allows us to take the risk of self-discovery.

SEXUALITY

> When touch is the Spirit's eloquence, the sexual embrace becomes the final sacramental escape from self-love (*The Courage To Be Married, op. cit.,* p. 118).

The liberation the Spirit works in Christian marriage extends to every facet of our life. This freedom is crystalized in a couple's sexual life. Perhaps we shouldn't consider sex as an aspect of our lives as much as we should consider ourselves sexual beings. We live a sexual life in marriage. You can't limit the sexual life to the bedroom. As most couples will readily tell you, "You can't be a grouch all day and expect to make love at night." Sexual intimacy is much more than intercourse; it is all the ways in which a couple express their love throughout their life together. Sex is the symbol of love, and without the lived reality the actions are meaningless.

Once I was on a retreat with Father Ken Sommers where he challenged the married couples to realize that spiritual intimacy is human "intimacy." How's your love life? Is it as exciting as it used to be? Are you joyful, creative and spontaneous lovers? Are you discovering love in discovering each other's bodies? Or is it a routine, a dull, plodding bore? Well, that's where you discover the selfishness and sin in your marriage. How joyful is your sexual life?

Sex is holy. The problem is that for so many marriages the holiness of sex connotes seriousness, boredom, and silence. Yet Paul says that this sexual love is a mystery foreshadowing the way Christ loves the Church. And if we read the Song of Songs we see a poem of the beauty and joy of erotic love.

> Let him kiss me with kisses of his mouth!
> More delightful is your love than wine.
> Your name spoken is a spreading perfume. . . .
> Ah you are beautiful, my beloved
> Ah, you are beautiful.
>
> Your eyes like doves
> behind your veil. . . .
>
> Your lips like a scarlet shroud;
> your mouth is lovely
>
> Your breasts are like twin fawns.
> Your rounded thighs are like jewels,
> the handiwork of an artist. . . .
>
> You have ravished my heart, my sister, my bride.
> You have ravished my heart

with one glance of your eyes.

(Song of Songs 1:1; 4:1, 3, 5, 9)

This explicit eroticism in the Song is most often seen as an allegory of God loving Israel. However, the Song was included in the Hebrew canon at least a century before there was an allegorical interpretation of it. It was accepted as an inspired portrayal of the goodness and joy of sexual love. (Cf. *The Promise To Love: A Scriptural View of Marriage* by Wilfred J. Harrington O.P.)

Christians have had a hard time integrating the joy of sex with the call to holiness. I guess sex always seemed too much fun to be holy, in line with Augustine's famous remark:

> In marriage, intercourse for the purpose of generator has no fault attached to it, but for the purpose of satisfying concupiscence (lust) provided with a spouse, because of the marriage fidelity, it is *but a venial sin.*

Alongside of this negativity to pleasure the Church had to battle to maintain that the body and sexuality are good. Many rigorist and charismatic heresies considered our bodies and sexuality impure, if not evil. For them, sex kept us from being holy, and the only really spiritual way was total abstinence. We are still overcoming the effects of this anti-sex prejudice.

The point I want to make is that sex is good and sexual pleasure is a way God makes us whole and holy human beings. The couples in our community have experienced this liberation to joy in sex, as their love and intimacy grew also.

> Our sexual life was in pretty poor shape mostly because of all the restrictions, patterns, fears, and guilt that we absorbed in our upbringing. Experiencing God's love together has really changed our sexual life. It has become more a gift of our self and less a matter of self-satisfaction. You know you are loved in a physical, mental and spiritual oneness that is constantly deepening.

Liberation in Jesus is human liberation which transforms and enriches our sexuality. We not only learn affection but creativity, spontaneity, and playfulness. This gift of sexual exuberance breaks down the social inhibitions and Christian images of dirty sex that kill intimacy. Through the power of the Spirit healing us of our guilt and anxiety we discover a sexual innocence and joy that reminds us of the paradise that God intended for us. Our sexuality is "reborn" in a new creation, freed from distortions and guilt.

Obviously this is not just a matter of learning techniques. Techniques are important insofar as beginning a free sexual relationship. Learning sexual techniques frees us from our sexual myths and prejudices. They are important in the same way that learning to read music is important to a musician. After a while, as you go on to be creative, they are there but forgotten and taken for granted.

Sexual expression is not just a matter of manipulating each other's bodies to orgasm. It is the expression of a unitive experience of love and intimacy. There is a mystical quality to these peak experiences where the physical union is caught up in a much more significant spiritual union of persons in love. That is why intercourse sometimes doesn't feel like it's enough for two lovers. They long for a total union, a complete interpenetration of spirits. In making love they experience the need for heaven.

Talking about peak experiences of sexual intimacy is not to disparage the everyday comfortableness of a great deal of our sexual lives. There is also real love in our mundane, matter-of-fact sexual experiences. However, most people don't need to be encouraged to have mundane sexual experiences. They will happen as a matter of course.

The whole point is that sexual love and pleasure is a large part of how Jesus brings joy and healing in marriage. This most impressed me when talking to a young father about how the ecstasy of sexual love is an image of the Kingdom of God:

Making love has taught me what it means to be a child of God. A child's life is simple, playful and full of discoveries. I can be all of this in making love with my wife. Here love releases in me this gift of spontaneity and wonders. I am learning to rejoice in what a *gift* love is. I can accept and delight in the pleasure my wife gives me. And I know that I don't have to perform to deserve this. I can see that she is happy just to give me pleasure and joy. Of course, the result of this is that I want to give her pleasure, not as a bargain, but simply because it makes me happy to see her happy.

Isn't this the way we should relate to God—to accept the love He gives us as a gift that makes Him happy? Shouldn't we enjoy His love, delight in His love? If we do this, then we are delighted in loving Him, simply to bring Him joy.

This is what sexual love is for me. It's a celebration of our joy and love, a celebration of our bodies. It's the first glimpse of the total oneness that is heaven.

MARRIAGE AND COMMUNITY

Christian marriage is in community, for community, and supported by community. And Christian marriage is a community. Marriage as a sacrament and charism is set within the context of the Church to build up the Church. As Rosemary Haughton describes it:

For marriage is not a private thing, it is not a legalized love affair. It only makes sense as part of the life of a community which is there to witness the promises, to support the couple in their growth and to provide the setting for their child's education—which is much more than mere schooling. . . .

Sexuality is a *quality of human community*. The coming together of two of the community in a permanent union is part of the growing of the community. The two bring to their union the values and customs of the community to found and enrich their union and they, by their love and their growing together, in their turn enrich the community. They need the community and the community needs them. This is why marriage, though it is intimate and in great measure a secret between two, cannot ultimately be private. It is a public act and a public service. This is why we celebrate weddings in church or in some other public place where the community can gather to witness the founding of a new family and wish it well and pledge its support. (*The Mystery of Sexuality*, Paulist Press, N.Y., 1972, p. 59).

PRACTICALITIES

The responsibilities of Christian marriage need to be coordinated with the responsibilities of love in a Christian community. Coordination does not mean equal time. Negatively it means that the needs of the community are not always subordinated to the needs of my marriage nor is my marriage always subordinate to the needs of the community. Neither one has absolute priority over the other. Rather I need to evaluate the needs of my community and my marriage and to decide week by week which has priority on my time. Sometimes I need to spend more time with the family; other times I should give more time to the community. Through mistakes and direction we gradually get a sense of balance and timing about our responsibilities.

In our group it usually works out that the family has the most pressing demand on our love. This is not a formula, but happens simply because *one person is usually more important to his family than to his larger community.* The family needs him more than the community does. For example, a family problem often needs immediate action (i.e., sickness, arguments, etc.). Community problems can rarely be solved in a night. In addition to these practicalities of love, there is what Thomas Aquinas calls the order of charity (agape). God gives me a responsibility to love some people more intensely than others. Family and friends should have a greater demand on my love simply because the depth of our relationship is a sign of how God wants me to love. These deep relationships need to be developed, and that takes time. To ignore the challenge to grow in these relationships for the sake of the community would be irresponsible.

What is needed is a lot of flexibility and understanding on both sides. Both community and marriage can be escapes from love. People can flock to prayer meetings the same way they used to "go out with the boys." More often, as our couples have experienced it, the family is a convenient excuse for avoiding community life.

THE NUCLEAR FAMILY
The American syndrome of togetherness is to build a world of their own and hide there. The breakdown of family ties and increased mobility has brought this about. The extended family of grandparents, aunts, uncles, etc., has broken down in favor of the nuclear family of the married couple and their children. While this eliminates some family squabbles, it forces the family to depend on itself for growth, entertainment, finances, etc. So each home becomes a self-contained community which the people never have to leave because everything is provided for right at home.

Obviously this impoverishes the family. Spouses are expected to fulfill each other's every need, and they find that they can't do it. So they watch television! Well, I'm getting overly simplistic. The point is that a normal person has more needs than his spouse can fulfill if he is to grow. Perhaps my wife hates politics and I find it a great source of self-discovery. Should I give up politics or should she be free enough to let me grow with others in this area of my life? What if she's having a problem that I don't seem capable of helping her to solve? Shouldn't she be able to be helped by someone else? Maybe we're just bored with each other and need some outside experience to help us grow. Obviously this can be done in a wrong way that amounts to psychological and spiritual adultery. However, the experienced reality remains: I need more than my spouse to make me a whole and holy person.

FRIENDSHIPS
What we've found is that this need for an extended family can be fulfilled in forming intimate Christian friendships. (Cf. Volume II.) This happens either individually or with the couple befriending another Christian couple. One such group of married friends has been praying together every week for over three years. It's absolutely amazing to see the depth of love that they share together. They have helped each other, fought together, and even

worked through a time when they liked each other's spouse better than their own. After all of this, they've reached the point where one of the men can say of the other, "I've never had a brother, but this man is closer to me than that. He knows *everything* about me and still he loves me. You know, sometimes I feel that my wife has to accept me because, well, she's married to me. But that this man loves me like that, well it's just fantastic."

Friendship opens up a marriage so that each partner can grow to his or her fullest. This, in turn, enriches the marriage. Another common benefit of these relationships is that a couple can honestly share and pray about their married life with their friends. The only caution here is that the depth of the friendship can never be greater than the depth of the marriage. It takes couples who are secure in their marriage to develop these kinds of relationships. Even though they can be dangerous, friendships outside the marriage provide the kind of sharing, perspective, and support that all couples need.

HOSPITALITY AND SERVICE

Marriage is also a charism for the community. Mostly this charism is in the witness of the love shared in the family. If the love is there, then it will naturally overflow to people outside the family. This means that the time, talents, and home of Christian families will be available to serve the community in love. This, of course, goes against the idea of a necessary privacy for the nuclear family. As Paul says:

> Love must be completely sincere. Love one another warmly as brothers in Christ and be eager to show respect for one another. . . . Share your belongings with your needy brothers and open your homes to strangers. (Romans 12 and 13—TEV)

It's all so simple—just "open your homes." This is one of the most impressive witnesses of the love of Christian marriage. Can you imagine what this country would be like if every home were a center of this hospitality and love? Children would learn by experience what it means to be loving and Christians when they saw their parents doing this. We'd probably rediscover the lost art of conversation and lose a little of the addiction to TV.

CHILDREN

This leads right into the whole subject of providing a Christian environment for children. Now I don't just mean education, I mean the whole environment of love and service. Christians (especially recently converted Christians) seem to spend too much time converting their children instead of loving them. Personally I think it's a far greater work of the Spirit that a child knows he is loved rather than forcing him to speak in tongues at twelve years old. This is an unconditional love which accepts the child for who he is even if he doesn't like the idea of Christianity. Of course, there is the responsibility to teach the child the faith, but this doesn't mean forcing him to accept what it took us thirty or forty years to believe. Anyway, forcing doctrine on children doesn't seem to work well. As Rosemary Haughton points out in her book *"It's a Living, Loving Thing,"* children tend to have childish ideas of the faith. What else would you expect? If they do remember any of our doctrine, they favor the bizarre distortions which are more interesting than orthodoxy. *What does affect children is the atmosphere of love and faith in the family.* If hospitality and love are taken-for-granted ways of doing things, that's what the child will learn. Children remember what we do more than what we say. It is our love more than our teaching that reveals the reality of God's love.

P.S.   THE IN-BETWEEN

There are many people who may feel alienated by this chapter. I am explicitly talking about marriages where both partners explicitly share their Christian faith. There are many other situations where people cannot realize this kind of marriage. These are those whose spouse is not Christian and those who are separated and divorced.

When a Christian and non-Christian are married, an enthusiastic faith in either partner can cause problems. It's basically a question of trying to reconcile two different value systems. You tend to get different answers to the same question. If either partner thinks of his or her spouse as "someone to be converted to the truth," you have even more problems. Again, the whole point of Christian marriage is to love unconditionally.

If you remember Keith Miller's story about his problems with who's to take out the garbage, there was a resolution to it. For years he tried to convert his wife, brought home books, tapes, etc., but the more he tried the more resistant she became to his holy-roller religion. Eventually he gave up. After a longer time, he finally realized that he was supposed to be loving his wife. So, he took out the garbage. And, as he did more and more loving things for her, she began to take notice of his Christianity. Because she finally saw a change in her husband, his Christian faith became literally believable. This is the basic way that spouses seem to be able to accept their partners' religion. Again, love speaks louder than words.

Most of the time these are situations where both partners are Christian but of different intensities and style. And in the long tradition of Christian in-fighting this can be a worse situation than an atheist—Christian marriage. What we have found is that if this was a good marriage to begin with, then one partner becoming an enthusiast will most likely enrich the marriage. If it's a bad marriage, then chances are it can get worse.

In the good marriages (with Christian and non-Christian both) we found that if a couple regularly shares about their religious commitment, things work out. In a few cases, the non-involved spouses ended up knowing more about our community than some of the members did. The key here is to respect each other's religious commitment. It also helps if the couple can get to know the people in each other's religious groups. Hopefully, this goes a long way to dispelling any ideas that "my mate is going around with a bunch of kooks."

In terms of charismatic communities, this loving communication is especially important. If anything, charismatic groups are at least different, and most people need to get familiar with the whole idea before they plunge in. This happened in a really beautiful way with one deeply Christian couple. As in most cases, the wife came home speaking in tongues one day. Even though she never verbally pushed her husband, the force of her exuberance and involvement strained their relationship to the point of making it a living hell. He felt that for the first time in their life they were walking down different roads. Eventually the wife reached the point of realizing that her family was her primary commitment in the Lord. At this point of renunciation she told her husband that she would give up all her involvement for the sake of the marriage. He then admitted that he had no right to stop her from following the Lord the way she felt He wanted her to. He was following the Lord the way he thought was right, and she should do the same, and that changed everything. Over the next five years, he became friends with a number of people in the community. Even though he finds the charismatic community not quite his style, he is more passionate in defending us and publicizing us than many of the members. He even gave a talk at a conference with one of our teams. His first words were "Even if I'm not a tonguer, I want to tell you how a traditional Catholic follows the Lord being married to a charismatic."

THE DIVORCED STATE

Divorced Catholics are, in practice, living a life of celibacy. And without getting into a discussion on remarriage, I want to describe some ways the Spirit can work in the divorced state.

The first thing would be to check with the parish priest about the possibility of an annulment. The process here has become greatly simplified, and if there is a desire for marriage, the technicalities should be checked out.

Secondly, we've seen community life become a place of meaning and fullfilment for divorced people. Normally the divorced end up terribly lonely. They no longer fit in with their married friends. Divorced people are often considered dangerous for married couples to befriend. Somehow they're thought of as always out to get another man or woman.

However, in our community we've witnessed just the opposite. Divorced people are welcomed into sharing both with married and with single people. There is a tremendous sense of freedom where they feel that they can love without fear. It might seem a little unusual to have a husband having lunch with his wife's divorcée friend, but that's what can happen when people can love in the strength of their relationship with God. This is a healing love where divorced people can overcome the scars of a bad marriage and learn again to trust and love.

In all of this we are discovering wholly new potentials for Christian marriage. People are discovering themselves and their spouses in new and exciting ways. There is in community a wholly different style of life for married couples. A Christian couple is not left to their own devices to work out their marriage. There is the love and help of friends and the support of a wider community to serve as an extended family. Prayer, sacraments, and spiritual direction are further aids to learn how to love.

We have only begun to realize the implications of this kind of Christ-centered marriage. Basically, it gives a vision of spouses loving each other with a free, unconditional love, supported by the power of God through prayer and community. There is a sense of beginning an adventure of love which is to actualize this mystery and symbol of Christ's love for the Church.

CELIBACY

One of the life-style options that has existed in the Christian community from the beginning is the celibate life. In plain language, the Christian celibate is one who refrains from marriage because that is what he or she feels called by God to do.

There are many reasons for remaining unmarried. Some people do it simply because they have not been asked or accepted. Others do it so they can be freer to do what they want. Others refrain from marriage because they are so busy with their work that they do not think it would be fair to the one they might marry. Some are afraid that they could not make it work, or that they could not handle the responsibility. I am sure there are lots of other reasons.

The Christian celibate refrains from marriage simply because he or she feels called by God to do so. It is not an escape. It is not a denial of the goodness of sexuality or the goodness of marriage, although people in the past have given these reasons. The Church has declared those doctrines heretical because they grow out of the error that anything to do with the body or with the world is evil. The Church has always been strongly in support of the bibli-

95

cal perspective that we and the world are God's creation and are good. Various Christian writers at different times have spoken negatively about sex and marriage, but they were simply wrong.

In the Gospel of Matthew we find Jesus responding to a question about divorce, which provokes the disciples to suggest that perhaps it is better not to marry. And Jesus replies:

> Not everyone can accept this teaching, only those to whom it is given to do so. Some men are incapable of sexual activity from birth; some have been deliberately made so; and some there are who have freely renounced sex for the sake of God's reign. Let him accept this teaching who can (Matthew 19:11-12).

A more literal translation would be "because of" rather than "for the sake of" God's reign, and the force of Christ's teaching would more accurately be: because people have been touched by the reign of God, they are celibate.

I said earlier that celibacy has existed in Christianity from the beginning because Jesus and some of his followers were celibate. Some of the people of the Qumran community (source of the Dead Sea Scrolls) seemed to have practiced celibacy, but it was a very odd thing among the Jewish people of the time of Jesus for them to see this itinerant band with Jesus refraining from marriage. Jesus' explanation is: The reign of God has touched them. It's not for everyone, but for those who are so called. They are a gift to the community.

Jesus simply describes the situation. He uses the declarative form of the verb, not the exhortative or prescriptive form. He gives no exhortation or command, which Paul alludes to in I Corinthians 7:25: "With respect to virgins, I have not received any command from the Lord. . . ." The point is that Jesus offers no other reason than to say that it has happened. It is a sign that the end times have come and that the reign of God is at work among us. Since that time, other men and women have felt that same call.

There is no way that we can interpret such a call as a call to a better way of life than marriage as a way of following God's will. The sacrament of marriage is itself a sign that God's reign is among us. Once again, the fact that the calls are different does not make one better than the other.

In I Corinthians 7:32-35 Paul says:

I should like you to be free of all worries. The unmarried man is busy with the Lord's affairs, concerned with pleasing the Lord; but the married man is busy with this world's demands and occupied with pleasing his wife. This means he is divided. The virgin, indeed any unmarried woman, is concerned with things of the Lord, in pursuit of holiness in body and spirit. The married woman, on the other hand, has the cares of this world to absorb her and is concerned with pleasing her husband. I am going into this with you for your own good. I have no desire to place restrictions on you, but I do want to promote what is good, what will help you to devote yourselves entirely to the Lord.

Paul's words here are an often quoted rationale for claiming the superiority of celibacy over marriage, but that is just not the case. No one would be more upset by that interpretation than Paul himself. In so many places and so many ways Paul insists that everything is changed by Jesus and the coming of the Holy Spirit, and that every way of life is made holy by the Spirit. The context in which Paul writes makes it clear that he is concerned about Jesus coming soon (so why get involved in marriage?) and by the obvious advantage of not having the cares of marriage so that one may have more time and not be "divided" by those cares.

We cannot say that caring for one's wife and family and work are not capable of being sanctified by the Spirit, any more than we can say that "secular" activities of the celibate are not capable of being sanctified by the Spirit. We must not make the mistake of thinking that only directly religious activities such as prayer and preaching are holy, while everything else is secular. The holy is that which is animated by the Spirit, so all that is involved in marriage can be holy and is important for the renewal of the earth by the Spirit. The same is true of the work and play of the celibate, who may be freer to do religious things, but not holier because of it. The point is that each calling of the Lord allows us to draw close to Him, so it is not a matter of being better or worse, but different. The concept that sanctified marriage is indeed a light to a world in which bad marriages abound and that there are many married people numbered among the saints just highlights the fact that the Spirit sanctifies us in every way of life.

The Lord does say that the calling to celibacy is a gift, a charism, and we remember that all charisms are given, not because of holiness, but for the building up of the Body of Christ. The usual lifestyle of most of us involves marriage. That there are celibates reminds us that God's reign has broken in among us, if only because of the oddity of the unmarried man or woman. Of course, the force of sexuality in human life has always been powerful, so it is a great puzzle to many that anyone could remain celibate or would even want to. All things considered, there is a witness to the power of God in the celibate life.

I think it is also the case that celibates are freer for service, and in that sense are a gift to the community. I am not talking about the service of witness or of holiness, but of time available to give to others. Again, this in no way implies an advantage of holiness, but only of availability.

All of this rather lengthy discussion has only been elaborated for the sake of underlining the fact that celibacy is a viable life-option if the Lord so calls.

The celibate life is meant to be lived in the context of and for the sake of the Christian community. The fact of the calling most certainly does not mean that one becomes sexless, without desire or temptation, nor does it mean that intimate relationships are excluded. The calling itself grows out of the experience of God's call, and so a life in the Spirit is the context of that call. To attempt a celibate life because it is attached to the priesthood or religious life without the experience of intimacy with God is to assume a tremendous burden, and that does not represent the charism. The experience of God's presence and love serves to give the celibate the awareness of being loved or lovable, the only antidote to his or her aloneness. It is also the strength from which the choice is made.

In the context of the Christian community alive in the Spirit, all that is available to bring strength and holiness to all the members is available to the celibate. A continuing habit of honesty with himself and others, including his spiritual director, is a fundamental antidote to bad motives in relationships. The love of brothers and sisters is both healing and supportive and supplies the affection we all need. Prayer together, especially with intimate friends, keeps Jesus as the Lord of the relationship, and everyone grows deeper in the Lord. One of the greatest problems of living the celibate life is the weakness from past experiences of rejection. When the experience of the Lord's love and the affectionate relationships with brothers and sisters do not suffice to heal the need for affirmation, the community provides inner healing through its ministry.

Celibacy, then, like marriage, should be chosen out of strength, not out of weakness. The calling comes and is confirmed over a period of trial in the midst of the community. Then, after consultation with a spiritual director, one may feel that the call has been tested and that it is safe to follow that path.

POSTSCRIPT

In the past a great deal has been written about celibacy, and the life-styles of priests and religious have been very much influenced by the tone of that writing. It really is not worth the trouble to go into it all, but it is worth observing that much of what was written and much of the approved life-style of celibates was dictated by fear. Everyone seemed afraid that the priest or religious would run off and get married. Once the restrictions were relaxed in the sixties, a lot of them did, which says a lot about the inadequacy of the preparation for such a calling and the right kind of environment for growth in inner strength. All of that is changing now, thank God, but one final word should be said.

Fear is not a motive worthy of a Spirit-filled person. That certainly does not mean that, from time to time, if I am afraid, I should feel guilty. We have dealt with that elsewhere. But the point here is that whole programs of formation and the life-styles of celibate people should not be dictated by fear. Of course sexuality is a powerful drive. Of course it is risky to develop intimate relationships, especially with members of the opposite sex. But whenever I hear that I think of the time when I first began to work with horses. One of the men who worked there said to me, "Horses are powerful. If they kick you they could break a bone or even kill you. So respect their strength, but don't be afraid of them."

The call to celibacy is not a call which requires one to live only at the level of functional relationships, absorbed in service, impersonal in the deepest sense of that word. Just the opposite is true. Armed with all sources of strength described earlier, the celibate, like every other Christian, is called to love and to friendship. We do not need to be afraid, but we do need to be careful.

The Lord has blessed me over the years with very close friends of both sexes. Only through these relationships have I learned anything at all about non-possessive, non-coercive love. Only through them has my deep selfishness been exposed so that it could be forgiven and healed. Only through them have I known the crucifixion of love which leads to resurrected love. Yes, there has been pain. Yes, there has been deep joy. Thank God for it all. Thank God for His Spirit and the understanding of loving brothers and sisters who gave us support in the conviction that we never have to give up, that we can work through all our problems.

BIBLIOGRAPHY

RECOMMENDED READING:

Champlin, Joseph M., Fr., *Do You Love Me?*, Ave Maria Press, Notre Dame, Indiana, 1968, 207 pp.

A good balanced book on dating and pre-marital sex and love. Fr. Champlin gives a good solid presentation of Church teaching with a very compassionate look at contemporary problems of morality.

Hanaghan, Jonathan, *The Courage To Be Married*, Abbey Press, St. Meinrad, Indiana, 1974, 133 pp.

A great book that grips you with the authenticity of the author's experience. It's basically a series of reflections on marriage from a wise and learned old man. It does not pretend to give the whole picture on marriage, but it's more a series of poignant in-

sights. The middle chapters might be too much of Freud for the average reader.

Powell, John, *The Secret of Staying in Love*, Argus Communications, Niles, Ill., 1974, 188 pp.
   Like Powell's other books, Why Am I Afraid to Tell You Who I Am? *and* Why Am I Afraid to Love? *this latest work focuses in on the need for honest dialogue and communication between partners. Very practical and experiential, the book includes follow-up exercises to help make dialogue a regular part of married life.*

Schillebeeckx, Edward, O.P., *Marriage: Human Reality and Saving Mystery*, Sheed and Ward, New York, 1966 (2 vols.), 415 pp.
   A beautifully written and exhaustive scholarly treatment of Christian marriage. The scope includes a thorough analysis of marriage in the Old and New Testaments and a study of marriage throughout the history of the Church. It is especially good for understanding the cultural roots of Christian marriage (i.e., male headship).

SUPPLEMENTARY READING:

Harrington, Wifred J., O.P., *The Promise of Love: The Scriptural View of Marriage*, Alba House, Staten Island, New York, 1968, 141 pp.
   If you don't have time for Schillebeeckx, this will give you the scriptural essentials without an historical perspective. Good perspective on love and sexuality.

Haughton, Rosemary, *It's a Living, Loving Thing*, Ave Maria Press, Notre Dame, Indiana, 1970, 141 pp.
   A delightful and challenging book that explodes a lot of adult fantasies about Christian education. If you want to know what children actually learn about Christianity, this book will both surprise and humble you. Should be required reading for all charismatic parents.

————, *The Mystery of Sexuality*, Paulist Press, New York, 1972, 77 pp.

A nice little book that cuts through the pious clichés to look at the human, spiritual realities of sexuality. This book is a good balance to the narrowness of sexual manuals in that it describes sexuality as integrated with the whole mystery of human life.

O'Neill, George and Nena, *Open Marriage*, Avon Books, New York, New York, 1972, 286 pp.

An immensely popular book that came along with the right idea at the right time. Because of this, half the book is wasted on polemics against traditional ideas of marriage. However, the basic ideas of an open-ended marriage relationship can easily be incorporated into the context of a Christian community. While many parts of this book can be, so to speak, "baptized," some elements (like experimental adultery) should obviously be ignored.

Wyden, Peter, and Bach, George, R., Dr., *The Intimate Enemy, How To Fight Fair in Love and Marriage*, Avon Books, New York, New York, 1968, 382 pp.

Very practical book within the limitations of its topic. Because of this intense focus on conflict there is a tendency to take this book too seriously as a magical solution to all marital problems.

by Anthony Cushing

The Mission of the Church 4

As the Father has sent me, so do I send you. . . . You will be witnesses to me (John 20:21; Acts 1:8).

We are to love as Jesus loves. We are called to be servants, to give our talents and time to transform the world. The Church is to witness Jesus to the world through our preaching, our unity and our love. In this we have to trust in the guidance and power of the Spirit among us. However, this still leaves a number of questions to be answered. How does my service relate to the local church? How does the work of our prayer group tie in to the mission of the parish and the universal Church? Which projects demand our time commitment? What is a Christian attitude toward "the world"?

Obviously, all these questions cannot be answered for particular situations. What I hope to do is to describe some general principles to help discern what God is asking of us in our particular situations.

THE MISSION OF THE CHURCH IS ECCLESIAL

Sometimes I get frightened when I think that I am to love and serve as Jesus loved. And this fright comes from a realization of how great the problems are and how inadequate I am to the task. I can just about cope with my own problems. How am I supposed to be a "light to the world"? When I feel this way it's great to realize that I am not alone in this work of love. There are all the people in any community in the parish and in the universal Church who are called to be lovers just as Jesus was. Together, in

103

the Spirit, we are to be Christ's presence in the world. I am a part of that great body of believers and saints. I have a job to do, but it is a small part of the great work of the church.

There are a number of implications to saying that the work of the Church is ecclesial. In the first place it means that my individual gifts are to be coordinated in love with the needs and direction of my community. In our life *together* we are a witness to Jesus' love and power. Christians have a mission as a people; we are saved as a people. That means that I don't have to participate in every function and service of the Church.

I remember reading the witness of a Protestant minister which illustrates this rather clearly. For years he had been trying to meet all the needs of his people—praying, counseling, administrating, ministering to the sick, etc. Then, finally, it occurred to him in prayer: "I am not the whole Church. I am a member of the Church. There are other people whom God wants to use in service. Anyway I just can't take it anymore. I'm exhausted." As soon as he realized this, the people in his church had a chance to use their gifts in service. For each of us to realize that "I am not the whole Church" is to trust that our fellow Christians will respond to God's Spirit to bring forth a diversity of gifts in the unity of the Body. As Paul states in Ephesians 4:4-7, 16:

> There is one body and one Spirit. There is one Lord, one faith, one baptism, there is one God and Father of all men, *who is Lord of all, works through all and is in all.* Each one of us has been given a special gift in proportion to what Christ has given. . . . Under his control all the different parts of the body fit together and the whole body is held together by every joint with which it is provided. *So when each separate part works as it should the whole body grows and builds itself up through love.*

For each of us there are limitations of time, talents and resources to our service in the Church. There are so many needs, problems, and opportunities for doing good that I cannot possibly do them all. I have to make some concrete choices about what to do with my time. For example, I feel that God wants me to spend a good deal of my time writing. There are also many other good things I could be doing. It is a good thing to spend a lot of time getting to know the new people in the community. But if I am to be faithful to God's calling in my everyday responsibilities, I simply cannot spend a lot of time with new people (if I also want to sleep). This bothers me sometimes, but I simply have to trust that other people in the community will be doing what I cannot do.

There are also many other good services, organizations, and programs outside the community that I could get involved with. However, because I am committed to this group of people doing this particular service, the work of the community has a priority on my time and talents. This does not mean that I cannot get involved with services outside my community, it simply means that my community has the priority.

UNION WITH THE UNIVERSAL CHURCH

The broader perspective on my service is that it is to be coordinated with the mission of the entire Church. This means the Church as a visible, structured, historical group of people with definite leadership, teaching, and goals. As a Roman Catholic this means that I must attune myself to what the Spirit is saying in and through the Church. I have a responsibility to find out what the Church teaches, and to obey (listen and say "yes" to) that teaching. What are my leaders (pope, bishop and pastor) calling me to do in the Church? Listening to and responding to the Church leadership is a basic way that the Spirit directs and focuses my service.

There is a tendency in Charismatic Renewals to think of a "spiritual Church." What people mean by this is that they will listen to only the "true believers," "reborn and Spirit-baptized" Christians. As Ronald Knox said:

> The Enthusiastic works to see results; he is not content to let the wheat and the weeds grow side by side until the harvest. It must be made possible somehow, even in this world, to draw a line between the sheep and the goats. Thus a little group of devout souls isolates itself from the rest of society to form a nucleus for the New Jerusalem; and in doing so it

loses touch with the currents of thought that flow outside, and grows partisan in attitudes, sterile of new ideas. (*Enthusiasm*, Oxford: Clarendon Press, 1949, 1961, p. 229)

In addition to this kind of stagnation, the idea of a "spiritual Church" goes against the meaning of the Incarnation. Jesus was born into and lived in a particular historical society with the advantages and limitations of that society. The Church too has grown in a particular society, in history, with all the glories and disadvantages of each age. Scripture gives evident witness that the work of Jesus was carried on by a real historical community. Very early the Church developed offices, structure, and "sound doctrine." The Church is a visible, historical structure because it is a human necessity to have structure for people to live and work together for a common purpose. The Spirit works in these visible, tangible, mundane realities, not just in the inner man. And the Spirit works in ordinary believers who might not have "charismatic enthusiasm." Charismatics need to listen and learn from all the ways that the Spirit is working in the Church. Especially in the areas of liturgy, Scripture, theology, and marriage, the Charismatic Renewal is too new and too narrow to have much to offer here. There is much to learn from people critical of the Charismatic Renewal. They bring a much needed light to our many weaknesses and help us maintain a healthy balance. In any case, to listen only to those who agree with us is the surest way to develop a narrow mind.

To be united to the universal Church is to have at my disposal the wisdom, witness, and mistakes of 2,000 years of Christians. Of course, many people do not see the Church this way. They limit their vision of the Church to the very ordinary people I meet on Sunday. They don't seem to have much brilliance or enthusiasm. I think most people who reject the Church do not do so after studying its theology and history. Usually people reject the Church because they have had a bad experience with the members and/or clergy of the Church. This is a very understandable mistake.

This temptation to avoid the help of the Church is described in a section of *The Screwtape Letters*, where a leading devil writes to his "nephew" devil on how to tempt a newly converted assignment:

One of our (devils') great allies at present is the Church itself. Do not misunderstand me. I do not mean the Church as we see her spread out through all time and space and coated in eternity, terrible as an army with banners. That, I confess, is a spectacle which makes our boldest tempters uneasy. But fortunately it is quite invisible to these humans.

All your patient sees is the half-finished, sham Gothic erection on the new building estates. When he goes inside, he sees the local grocer with rather a holy expression on his face bustling up to offer him one shiny little book containing a liturgy which neither of them understands, and one shabby little book containing corrupt texts of a number of religious lyrics, mostly bad, and in very small print. When he gets to his pew and looks around him he sees just that selection of his neighbors whom he has hitherto avoided. You want to lean pretty heavily on those neighbors. Make his mind flit to and fro between an expression like "the body of Christ" and the actual faces in the next pew. It matters very little, of course, what kind of people that next pew really contains. You may know one of them to be a great warrior on the Enemy's (Jesus') side. No matter. . . . Provided that any of those neighbors sing out of tune, or have books that squeak or double chins, or odd clothes, the patient will quite easily believe that their religion must therefore be somehow ridiculous. At his present stage, you see, he has an idea of "Christians" in his mind which he supposes to be spiritual but which in fact is largely pictorial. His mind is full of togas and sandals and armour and bare legs, and the mere fact that the other people in church wear modern clothes is a real—though of course unconscious—difficulty to him. Never let it come to the surface, never let him ask what he expected them to look like. . . . Work hard, then, on the disappointment or anti-climax which is certainly coming to the patient during his first few weeks as a Churchman.

I have been writing hitherto on the assumption that the people in the next pew afford no *rational* ground for disappointment. Of course, if they do—if the patient knows that the woman with the absurd hat is a fanatical bridge player or the man with squeaky boots a miser and an extortioner—then your task is so much the easier. *All you then have to do is to keep out of his mind the question "if I, being what I am, can consider that I am in some sense a Christian, why should the different sides of those people in the next pew prove that their religion is mere hypocrisy and convention?"* (*The Screwtape Letters*, Macmillan, N.Y., 1961, pp. 12-13).

The problem then is not the Church but my judgment of the faith and character of the people I encounter. Perhaps we should do what we pray in the Mass and "look not on our sins but on the faith of your people."

What we need to learn is what it means to belong to the Church triumphant. There is a tremendous amount of security in this. I am united not only with the Church on earth but with the communion of saints throughout time. All the great heroes (and everyday heroes) of ages past are praying with me and offering me encouragement to persevere in love and service. This became very real to me one time when I had to give a seminar and was marvelously depressed. Driving over in the car I started singing the litany of the saints. Suddenly I had this picture of Mary, Paul, Peter, Francis, Benedict, Anthony, all present with me. I could almost hear Benedict saying: "Don't give up. We all felt this way at one time or another. Jesus will take care of you." And He did. It's nice to know that even though I will often fail, "the gates of hell shall never prevail against the Church."

Practically, this listening to the Church is to help form my priorities about how I should be spending my time. Also, this liberates me from having to feel that I have to get involved in every service. There are mammoth problems of poverty and injustice that make me feel impotent and confused as to what to do. And my prayer group and parish can do very little for such mammoth problems. However, this is part of the mission of the entire Church. Sometimes the most I will be able to give is prayer and what money I can spare. Perhaps my parish can reach out in more concrete ways to alleviate the social injustices in our own area. However not every Christian or every community is specifically called to a ministry of social action. There are many groups (religious orders, agencies, and prayer groups) that are called to concentrate on that area. However, that does not mean that I must involve myself if I feel God calling me to serve in another way.

This is basically a question of discerning in what direction the Lord wants us to go. There is a long tradition in the Church that different groups or spiritualities have different ministries. The Franciscans live and work in a much different way than the Jesuits. Contemplative monks and sisters do not frequently engage in a social action program. The Church has always felt that this kind of diversity is not only permissible but healthy for the Church. Similar to individual Christians, each community "has been given a special gift in proportion to what Christ has given" (Eph. 4:7) to build up the universal Church in love.

THE WITNESS OF THE COMMUNITY

You are the light of the world. A city set on a hill cannot be hidden. Men do not light a lamp and then put it under a bushel basket. They set it on a stand where it gives light to all in the house. In the same way, your light must shine before men so that they may see goodness in your acts and give praise to your heavenly Father. (Matthew 5:14-16)

Go, therefore, and make disciples of all the nations. Baptize them in the name of the Father and of the Son and of the Holy Spirit. Teach them to carry out everything I have commanded you. (Matthew 28:19-20)

Both of these sayings of Jesus primarily concern the mission of the universal Church. My particular community is a very small light and would find it difficult to teach even Allentown. However these sayings gives us a sense of perspective about what our communities should be doing. Our first task is to *be* a community, to be a light of Jesus' love and presence. This in itself is a tremendous work of the Spirit. People need to have a place where they can see the Gospel lived and made real in the love of a group of people. Simply to lead the kind of life where people would say "Look at how they love one another" is the major task of a Christian community.

This community witness of love is desperately needed in this society where everyone is selling something. What with the barrage of advertising, most people find it very difficult to believe anything that sounds like a sales pitch. Very often when I talk to someone about Jesus I end up saying: "Come and see the community." People need to see how Jesus can change people's lives. An individual Christian can be just a nice guy or a "weirdo," so very often people need to experience Christians praying, working, and playing, for the Good News to be believable.

In our own community most of our witness is in just being a community. People hear about us from a friend or their priest, or they simply stop by out of curiosity. We don't really need a program to recruit people. People just come and we keep thankfully wondering how they got there. The presence of a Christian community is often enough of a witness to attract people.

It is in the context of community that a lot of what would normally be called social action takes place. People with psychological problems are counseled. The sick and the lonely are comforted and often healed. Marital problems are worked out. Many people discover hidden talents and can, through the help they receive, begin productive lives of service to others. This is all a by-product of becoming involved in a loving and healing community. People's lives are transformed by love and the power of the Spirit. And, I suppose, that's a fairly good description of social action.

Practically, then, each Christian does not have to be always out evangelizing someone. Living a life of love will usually attract enough attention. This kind of witness is very familiar to most Catholics. It is easily the most dignified way to witness, for there is always dignity in silence and service. And this is particularly the kind of witness that most impressed Catholics. The Focolare movement of close to a million people is so taken with this witness of community that they almost refuse to verbally evangelize. They insist that people live with them to experience the love of the brothers. Charismatics have a lot to learn from this witness of love.

WITNESSING—HOW AND WHY?

Along with all I've said about the value of community witness, Christians should be willing and able to personally witness to what Jesus means to them. This is another sensitive topic for many Christians. There is a tremendous variety of styles of evangelizing, depending on how a particular community understands the Christian life. Some styles are very aggressive and seem to deny to a non-believer both intelligence and freedom of choice. More often than not this kind of proclaiming the Good News ends up in an argument. Other styles of witnessing are so timid as to leave people wondering why there is all the fuss about Jesus. What we need is to integrate boldness and sensitivity to lovingly witness and be Good News to the world.

As Peter says: "Be ready at all times to answer anyone who asks you to explain the hope you have in you. But do it with gentleness and respect" (1 Peter 3:16—TEV).

FIRST OF ALL, LOVE

We are called to love people, not convert them. To love as Jesus loves is to accept people for who they are, where they are. If I consider a person as "someone to be converted" then I am really not accepting that person. It is saying, "I will totally accept and love you only when you are a Christian the way I am a Christian." Witnessing is a way of loving someone. Because I love you I want to share with you the best treasure I have, and that is Jesus. As St. Augustine said in his treatise on Christian instruction: "Our human love is the vehicle for God's love." People most respond to the Good News when we are Good News to them.

Love creates a certain style of witnessing. If I love this person, then I do not try to coerce them to fit the mold I have in mind for them. Sharing the Good News of Jesus is offering them love which they can either accept or reject. It is important that we always give people the right and freedom to make up their own minds.

THE LANGUAGE OF LOVE

The best way to do this is to share how I have experienced Jesus changing my life. Very often if you tell people what they should believe or what's wrong in their lives, you'll only end up in an argument. This is especially true when telling already faithful Christians that they are "not really following the Lord" and "have to be baptized in the Spirit to be a real Christian." This only irritates people who feel that their faith is being judged. It would definitely irritate me. It also leaves the door open to a great argument. "Why do I have to do this? I'm a good Catholic." Anytime you inflict your beliefs on someone (politics, religion, art) you're headed for a conflict. The reason for this is that beliefs aren't so much intellectual conclusions as they are personal choices based on experience. This is why non-converted people can't make sense out of a converted language. They simply haven't had the same experience that the converted have. Redemption is a meaningful and powerful word to the believer. It describes a very rich and mysterious experience. For the nonbeliever it lacks that sting of meaning and probably refers more to Green Stamps than happiness. People really can't agree as to how great the Charismatic Movement is until they have some positive experience of it.

If, in love, you share with a person your experience of Jesus, then you completely avoid arguments. A person cannot argue with your experience. They can't say that that didn't happen to you. If you say that accepting Jesus has made you feel loved and integrated, then they have to accept it insofar as they consider you believable. Either it happened or you're insane. To say "This is what helped me" is to give people the freedom to accept or reject what you are offering. Also this kind of witnessing avoids the whole realm of "what you ought to do" and gives people the hope of what can happen if they want Jesus.

The whole business of understanding the limitations of "converted language" has a lot to do with the dynamics of loving communication. Loving communication means that *I speak for your sake, I put your interests and needs ahead of the way I like to do things*. That is, I use the kind of language *you understand* whether or not it is a Christian or converted language. Obviously, then, set routines and formulas are not the way to tell people about Jesus. Accepting the Good News is not parroting a set formula. Repentance is not a "fill in the blank" question; it is a matter of choice and love. Very often people cannot hear the Good News because a Christian's language doesn't make sense to them.

This is especially true in terms of Catholics "hearing" the message of the Charismatic Renewal. Charismatics often use a Pentecostal jargon that alienates faith-filled traditional Catholics. Our pastor has a motto about this: "Don't wave Pentecostal red flag words in front of the traditional bulls." People don't have to be "baptized in the Spirit"; they can understand a "personal renewal of baptism," a "release of the Spirit," a "prayer experience of the Holy Spirit." The message of the Charismatic Renewal needs to be translated into a Catholic language for Catholics so that people do not feel that they are getting involved in a new religion. This sensitivity to a person's religious tradition has to entail a respect and appreciation of the goodness in that tradition. This was brought home to me one time when I was going to try to charismatize a beautiful elderly lady with whom I had been going to daily Mass. "Mrs. _____, did you ever try speaking in tongues?" "No," she said. "Did you ever try the rosary?" Well up until that point I hadn't. So I tried it and Mary started to take a greater place in my life with God. I still don't know if that woman speaks in tongues, but she sure helped me get closer to God.

Proclaiming the Good News in a language that people can understand and being sensitive to their needs is what St. Paul describes as "being all things to all men."

> I am a free man, nobody's slave, but I make myself everybody's slave in order to win as many as possible. While working with the Jews, I live like a Jew in order to win them. . . . In the same way when with the Gentiles I live like a Gentile. . . . Among the weak in faith I become weak like one of them, in order to win them. So I become all things to all men, that I may save some of them by any means possible (I Corinthians 9:19-22—TEV).

What I want to do now is to give some helpful hints about how to lovingly witness to Jesus. Most of these hints come from personal experience.

1. *Use everyday language.* A lot of people don't have a religious language that is meaningful to them. This is especially true in terms of people's awareness of their own sin. If someone doesn't have a relationship with God it will be very hard for him to see that he is "breaking God's law" or "offending God." Questions like "What would you change in your life?" "What would you like the world to be?" and "Did you ever want someone to love you for just being yourself?" point out the experienced need for God and the desire for a new life. The Good News makes sense when people can connect it as a real solution to their experienced needs and desires.

2. *Be yourself—admit weakness—focus on God's love.* We don't have to convince people that we're holy. Either they experience our holiness in our love, or our words won't change things. Most often people need to hear that someone understands and "knows what it's like" to be lonely or confused. If we give the impression that "I used to be a sinner like you but now I'm holy," we'll probably just make a person feel worse about himself. The big point to communicate is *"Now I know I am loved;* sure I still have problems, but I have seen some of them solved, and so now I have a lot of hope for the rest." This can be done in a very natural way. We don't have to plaster a smile on our face to show our joy. We can relate person-to-person and be "weak with those who are weak in the faith."

3. *Avoid morality and Church politics.* We don't have to prove to people that they're sinners or to convince them of a certain style of Christianity. Awareness of sin is something that grows on a person as he gets closer to God. A person will usually find it as difficult as we did to *want* to change deep patterns of sin. What's important in witnessing is to get others to *want* to get closer to God. In the same way, we don't have to humiliate a person's style of worship; maybe he never felt that his Church was dead. Maybe his traditional Church isn't dead. Here we have to avoid the temptation to think that the only real Christians are our kind of Christians.

4. *Make a friend, be a friend, introduce a friend to Jesus.* This is a Cursillo motto. The idea here is that it is easier for people to believe in the power of God once they experience how much

you love them. On our part this entails a real commitment of time and service. This runs contrary to the "hit and run" style of one-night witnessing. Rather we are to stick with a person, help him, be a friend to him, so that he can experience the reality of God's love in our love. This is to realize that evangelization is not just helping people to have a religious experience. Evangelization should lead people to a mature Christian life in community. This takes time. Recently an evangelistic crusade came to town, and in talking with the people we found out that they too had come to this conclusion. As a result they were training their people to stay with one person for a year. This is much more in line with Jesus' example with the Apostles. The numbers don't matter as much as the quality of Christian life.

5. *Be open to the power of the Spirit.* The Spirit constantly surprises us. Whenever I get an idea that this is *the* right way to witness, immediately something happens that shatters my little categories. Then I realize again that I'm not running the show. I can't bring people to the Lord; only the power of the Spirit can do that. My words don't matter so much. They can help or hinder the work of the Spirit—but what really matters is that God is touching that person. Sometimes I think I'm saying all the wrong things and a person ends up saying: "It's almost as though you were reading my mind; every question I thought of you answered before I could say anything." Call it what you will, word of wisdom or knowledge, it usually happens without my feeling anything extraordinary. It's always a surprise. I've found myself witnessing to people in gas stations, banks, dances, over a cash register in a store, and one time a guy even dragged me into a topless bar to "have a drink and talk this over." Some people are awed with the love of Jesus, others by the power of the charisms, and more than a few have gotten involved because they liked the people and saw community as a good way to live together. Always the "Spirit blows where he will" and we have to be flexible enough to follow his leading.

THE CHURCH AND THE WORLD

The mission of the Church is to witness God to the world in

115

love and power. As a result of her mission the Church is to radically transform society.

> Through the Son then, God decided to bring the whole universe back to himself. God made peace through his Son's death on the cross, and so brought back to himself all things, on earth and in heaven. (Colossians 1:20—TEV)

> The Church is Christ's body, the completion of him who himself completes all things everywhere. (Ephesians 1:23—TEV)

For the Church to be herself is a revolution. Because the revolution is love, it is so subtle that even Christians forget that the Spirit is to "renew the face of the earth." Is the Church part of the world or separate from it? Should we just ignore the world, waiting in hope for the day when "Christ is all and in all"? What is a Christian attitude toward the world?

"The Church . . . in Jesus Christ" (1 Thess. 1:1; Phil. 1:1): To understand the world we first have to understand what Paul means to be "in Jesus Christ." Fr. James Reese, O.S.F.S., of the Word of God Institute and a Scripture professor at St. John's University, says that this characteristic phrase "in Jesus Christ" describes the universal reality of Jesus' Resurrection. That Jesus rose from the dead is not only that he physically came back to life. In the Resurrection and Ascension Jesus takes on a universal relationship to all men of all time. In a very real way the whole earth, the whole universe, is "in Christ." In this way Paul's salutation to the Church in Thessalonica is like an address: "To the Church in Thessalonica in Asia, on the earth, in the universe, in God and in Jesus Christ." So in this sense all of the world (earth) is in the Church and the Church is "in Christ."

Now, in Scripture the word "world" is used in a number of ways. (1) God so loved the world that he gave his only Son (John 3). (2) Do not conform to the standards of the world (Romans 12). (3) Be witnesses . . . to the world (Acts 1). (4) Love not the world or anything that belongs to the world (1 John 3). Sometimes the word is used to describe society or the earth (1 and 3). But in the theological sense, the world (2 and 4) is seen to be mankind organized against God. The world is man's collective sinfulness. In this way John Mackenzie can say "The world is hostile to God but God is not hostile to the world." (*Dictionary of the Bible*, p. 943)

So in a very real way we have difficulties drawing boundaries around the Church. In terms of membership the Church is all those who have been baptized "into Christ." Yet the Spirit has been sent into the world and, "blowing where he will," unites all men who "seek you (God) with a sincere heart" (Canon IV). There are "anonymous Christians" who, through their desire for God and a life of love, are "in Christ" though they don't know him in fullness. In this sense the Church is co-extensive with society and the earth. The Body of Christ has no boundaries and at the same time the Church is always in tension with the world. The Church is the "leaven" to change the world and cannot "conform to the standards of the world."

This tension between the Church and the world is described as: *The Church is in the world but not of it.*

The Church in the world is involved with and affected by society. On one level this is to say that the insights of sociology, psychology, history and politics can validly describe the life of the Church. Of course, the Church is also susceptible to the politicizing, narrow-mindedness, and mistakes that characterize any society. From this we can see that the Church is in many ways tied to the culture in which she exists. This both helps and hinders the mission of the Church. For example, the same medieval Church that tolerated slavery produced an awesome beauty in religious art and community renewals.

The Church is a Church of human beings, human beings who are sinners as well as saintly. Even the holiest are subject to the particular narrow-mindedness of their environment and to all the varied historical and political forces that all men are subject to. Because the Church is immersed in the world (like leaven in dough) it must be very leery of using the world's solutions to problems. "Not by might nor by power but by my spirit, says the Lord." For example you can build Christian community in a number of ways. A very efficient model is the way the army creates community. They strip a person of the "old man" (clothes, hair, relationships) and make the "new man" conform to uniform ways of dress, speech, work and patterned relationships of authority. The ideal result is a group of people who think and act alike to a common purpose. However this is entirely accomplished through external, sociological forces. This option can make a Christian community into a group of Charismatic commandos. It is interesting to note how often the image of an army has been used to describe Christian community. As some contemporary communities demonstrate, the danger here is that the image tends to become reality.

That the Church is in the world is not just a negative influence. The Church can, first of all, *learn* from the world.

> She (the Church) is firmly convinced that she can be abundantly and variously *helped by the world* in the matter of preparing the ground for the Gospel. This help she gains from the talents and industry of individuals and from human society as a whole (*Constitution on the Church in the Modern World*, n. 40).

> Thanks to the experience of past ages, the progress of the sciences and the treasures hidden in the various forms of human culture, the nature of man himself is more clearly revealed and new roads to truth are being opened. These benefits profit the Church too, for from the beginning of her history she has learned to express the message of Christ with the help of the ideas and technology of various peoples, and has tried to clarify it with the wisdom of philosophers too (*Constitution on the Church in the Modern World*, n. 44).

The Church can use the tools and talents of the world to help build up the Body of Christ. Sometimes Christians who think of the world as entirely evil will forsake the use of any "natural wisdom." They desire a purely spiritual Church. And, by denying the goodness of man's humanity, they often fall prey to the evil natural forces they are trying to escape. The Puritans are a good example of this. They originally tried to escape the law-based "dead" churches, and ended up more legalized than the churches they came from. The point is that Christians are body and spirit. To disembody man is not to make him spiritual but to kill him. As Blake wrote: "Those who would make themselves Angels become Beasts."

The Church in the world sees creation as good. It is the way man uses nature and his creativity that can become evil. However, through the power of the Spirit Christians can use the things that selfish men can make evil and turn their use to the glory of God. To go back to our example of building community, we can use the external sociological forces (language, clothing, custom and order) to build community as long as we recognize that they are sociological tools. There is a tendency here to call custom "God's will." Then we end up with *the* Christian way to dress, speak, pray, etc. We can start to confuse uniformity with unity. This trap is to set up a Christian standard of behavior to which people must conform or else they are not Christian. (Again the Puritans are a good example.) With all these dangers in mind we can use these powerful tools to help us all too human Christians become one. What we need to do is to distinguish the central essence of the Good News from the form and culture in which it is expressed:

Although the Church has contributed much to the development of culture, experience shows that because of circumstances, it is sometimes difficult to harmonize culture with Christian teaching.

These difficulties do not necessarily harm the life of faith. Indeed they can stimulate the mind to a more accurate and penetrating grasp of the faith. For recent studies and findings of science, history and philosophy raise new questions which influence life and demand new theological investigation. . . .

For the deposit of faith, revealed truths are one thing. The manner in which they are formulated without violence to their meaning and significance is another.

In pastoral care, *appropriate use must be made not only of theological principles, but also of the findings of the secular sources, especially of psychology and sociology.* Thus the

119

faithful can be brought to love the faith in a more thorough and mature way (*Constitution on the Church in the Modern World*, n. 62; italics added).

THE CHURCH IS NOT OF THE WORLD

All of this positive affirmation of the goodness of the world needs to be balanced with the more fundamental reality that the Church is the Church because of the gift of God. The Church "seeks first the Kingdom of God," depends on God to make it a "holy people, a royal priesthood, God's own people, chosen to proclaim the wonderful acts of God, who called you from the darkness into his own marvelous light" (1 Peter 2:9—TEV). There is always a tension between Christians and the world because Christians cannot accept the world's values and solutions before God's. Christians cannot trust in their own efforts and creativity to make them holy; they realize that only the Spirit can do this. As a pilgrim people they can find no lasting security in the things of the world which are passing away (1 John 3). The world says that conformity, will power, order, and technology will bring peace and happiness. Christians realize that only loving God and neighbor can do this. The basis of the Church's existence is the power of the Spirit, not human wisdom (I Corinthians 2). Christians can go along with the world up to a point. There will always be a fundamental difference because Christians "trust in God, not men." (To be free from the power of the world does not mean that we forsake science, art, or technology. As we developed earlier in Volume III the basic way the world affects us is in our values and patterns of behavior. Specifically, "we do not conform to the standards" of greed, convenience, functionalism, salvation through achievement, and social and sexual roles.)

So, in the end result, the Church is *in* the world, influenced by and using the creativity of the world, but the Church is not *of* the world. It does not derive its values, power or security from the world but from God.

THE CHURCH: THE SPIRIT AND THE APOSTLES

After all of this we come around again to asking, "What is

the mission of the Church?" "How does the Church communicate the reality of Jesus risen to the world?"

Jesus came so that men might know and enter into the love He shares with the Father and the Spirit. He shared His experience of what it means to be Son so that we all might be sons, who through the power of the Spirit can, like Jesus, say "Abba, Father."

Now, how did Jesus try to communicate this relationship to men? He didn't write a book or leave a detailed set of instructions. He, first of all, lived a fully human life, and when it was time for Him to reveal Himself, most of His time was spent with the twelve men He wanted to carry on the message. He loved, preached, worked, healed, prayed, forgave, went to parties, suffered, died, and rose. Jesus' whole life was the revelation of the Good News. To carry on the revelation of His whole life *Jesus sent both the Spirit and the Apostles:* The Spirit "will teach you all things and bring to your remembrance all that I have said to you" (John 15:26). "He will guide you into all the truth. . . . He will glorify Me, for He will take what is Mine and declare it to you. All that the Father has is Mine; therefore I said that He will take what is Mine and declare it to you" (John 16:13-15). "You shall receive power when the Holy Spirit has come upon you; and you *shall* be my witnesses" (Acts 1:8). "He will bear witness to Me; and *you also* are witnesses, because you have been with Me from the beginning" (John 15:26-27). The Apostles also witness to who Jesus is. "He who hears you hears Me, and he who rejects you rejects Me and he who rejects Me rejects Him who sent Me" (I Thessalonians 10:16). "As the Father has sent Me even so I send you" (John 20:21). As Father Yves Congar points out:

> The one sent and the person sending are equal in dignity, which is expressed in the Aramaic word for sent, Saliah; the one sent represents the person of his maker and has the same authority; he is to be received in the same way as the maker himself, from whom he has a power of attaining and whose functions he exercises in his absence (*The Mystery of the Church*, Helicon Press, Baltimore, Md., 1960, p. 149).

It is extremely important for us to appreciate that the mission of the Spirit and the mission of Apostles are united in the Church, the Body of Christ, the Messianic Presence. Some people have expressed this as the Charismatic and institutional aspects of the Church. Whatever you call these different aspects we must remember that:

1. Both the Spirit and the Apostles are intended by Jesus to communicate His presence to men.
2. There is a union of the two which is also a dynamic tension which leads to growth.
3. This is the synthesis of the gift of God (Spirit) and the response of man (Apostle).

Schematically, the difference would look like this:

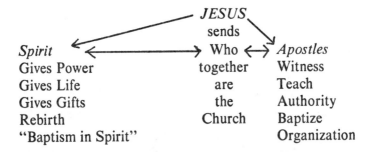

JESUS
sends

Spirit	Who ↔	*Apostles*
Gives Power	together	Witness
Gives Life	are	Teach
Gives Gifts	the	Authority
Rebirth	Church	Baptize
"Baptism in Spirit"		Organization

The best approach I've found as to how these two essential aspects of the Church interrelate is in Rosemary Haughton's book *The Transformation of Man*. She sees everyday life as a process of formation (parents, custom, law, education) which should lead to a transforming experience of love—hopefully through Christ but also through family, sex, politics, etc. Now the Church is for the formation of Christian values and life styles and to lead to transformation through the Spirit.

So our expanded scheme would present then two sides of the same form in the Church.

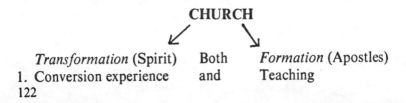

CHURCH

Transformation (Spirit)	Both	*Formation* (Apostles)
1. Conversion experience	and	Teaching

122

2. Powers to love and heal	and	Authority
3. Inspiration	and	Structure
4. Presence of God	and	Ritual and sacraments
5. Spontaneity, enthusi-asm, diversity	and	Discipline, organization, law and custom
6. Saints	and	Good men
7. Gift	and	Response

FORMATION for TRANSFORMATION

For Christians, *formation is to lead to transformation*

1. Teaching is to lead to conversion in the Spirit.
2. To be in authority is to open up to the powers of the Spirit to love and serve.
3. Structure is to lead us to the Spirit to be inspired as to God's will.
4. Ritual and sacraments are to bring us into the encounter with Jesus present in the Spirit.
5. Discipline is to lead to the enthusiasm of a transformed person.
6. Good men are to become saints by being filled with the Spirit.
7. Our response to God is to open us up to receive his gift of love.

A good example of this is trying to explain why someone should pray for a scheduled period of time every day.

Does taking time to pray change your life? Unless you are open to accept God's Spirit you could be on your knees an hour a day for fifty years and you still wouldn't be transformed. No amount of discipline or good habits can ever transform us to become saints. Only the Spirit transforms. Only the Spirit makes men saints. Yet if a person doesn't take the time to pray, the degree to which he's transformed will be significantly less. Taking time to pray is giving God a chance to transform our lives. The formation element of disciplining ourselves to prayer time is important insofar as it leads us to be transformed by God's Spirit.

123

God can transform us without the discipline but the formation discipline can never by itself transform us. However, the kind of formation we use will affect the depth and extent of the transformation that the Spirit works in us. Formation is like the earth and the Spirit's transformation is the seed. Earth can never produce a plant by itself, yet the health of a plant depends very much on the kind of earth where you place the seed. Formation is the dough that the yeast of the Spirit transforms. This is something of what Paul was teaching the Corinthians in the image of the Church as God's building:

> You are also God's building. Using the gift that God gave me, I did the work of an expert builder and laid the foundation and another man is building on it. But each one must be careful how he builds. For God has already placed Jesus Christ as the one and only foundation and no other foundation can be laid. Some will use gold, or silver, or precious stones in building on the foundation; others will use wood, or grass, or straw. And the quality of each man's work will be seen when the Day of Christ exposes it. For that Day's fire will reveal every man's work; the fire will test it and show its real quality. If what a man built on the foundation survives the fire, he will receive a reward. But if any man's work is burnt up then he will lose it, but he himself will be saved, as if he had escaped fire (I Corinthians 3:9-15).

Christian community is built upon each person's acceptance of Jesus Christ and openness to the transforming power of the Spirit. Without this foundation, community is not possible. Yet it takes more than a foundation to make a building. The teaching and pastoral care is the formation which is built upon the foundation of Jesus. What we build varies in quality according to our work. This has nothing to do with the salvation at the end time. The formation has to do with how much God's transforming power breaks into our lives. Jesus, the foundation, is essential; the formation and work that we provide determine how habitable God's building will be.

What we see in the Church at present and in the past is a great many parish communities trying to lead the Christian life without the foundation of repentance and being filled with the power of the Spirit. It may be a really beautiful building with good liturgy, social clubs, and social actions, but without faith-renewed Christians, it is not a vital Christian community. It may be an extremely habitable place—good order, everyone knows what to expect from each other, good things are being done—but the power of the Spirit has been diluted. You see everything but "God giving his Spirit and working miracles among you" (Galatians 3). Paul might say that their communities have been built with gold and silver without having a foundation.

At the same time we have many communities, usually in the evangelical and Pentecostal traditions, who very much experience the power of the Spirit through radical faith in Jesus. However, they have often lacked an awareness of the importance of formation, structure, theology, art, etc., to provide the fullest expression of God's Spirit. Very often these kinds of communities consider all normal human activity from parties to psychology as not "spiritual."

To understand this we have to look at the role of formation in the transformation (conversion) experience. The formation in which we are raised supplies us with answers to understand the world. However, for a lot of people that formation often breaks down in times of conflict and crisis. The old answers no longer work and we start looking for other solutions. The new solution can be anything—marriage, yoga, Marxism or God. This breakdown of the old formation (like the shell of a seed breaking) opens us up to be transformed by the power of love. This is like the old cliché: "There are no atheists in a foxhole." Why? Because in war the old answers to life and happiness are no longer relevant when confronted by the reality of a bullet. The security of a comfortable family doesn't solve that problem. This is also why so many people come to God after failure, because they now need God. This partially explains why there is a great spiritual renewal taking place in our culture now. All of the traditional values and answers to life have broken down, giving God a chance to break into our hearts.

Formation must break down for transformation to happen. Even very good, very religious formations must be broken. A good example is St. Paul. He describes himself in Philippians:

> If anyone thinks he can be safe in external ceremonies, I have even more reason to feel that way. . . . So far as the Jewish law is concerned, I was a Pharisee. . . . So far as a man can be righteous by obeying the commands of the law I was without fault. But all those things that I might count as profit I now reckon as loss, for Christ's sake. Not only those things. I reckon everything as a complete loss for the sake of what is so much more valuable, the knowledge of Christ Jesus my Lord. For his sake I have thrown everything away, so that I might gain Christ and be completely united with him. No longer do I have a righteousness of my own, the kind to be gained by obeying the law. I now have the righteousness that comes from God, and is based on faith (Philippians 3:4-9—TEV).

I wonder what Paul's mother thought of his conversion. Here he was—a good, obedient Jew, someone a mother could be proud of. As far as the Jew was concerned he was perfect. Yet all of that goodness had to go. Not that Paul started sinning. He gave up the security of his old answers. His old formation didn't lead to conversion but to more formation and law. So it had to go; it was just rubbish because it didn't lead to his being transformed by God. This was very difficult for Paul. He describes it as what later saints would call the "dark night of the soul." Our very identity is broken down so that we can be totally open to God's love. Inadvertently, this also explains why people from horrible backgrounds often find it easier to accept love than good people from disciplined formations.

This idea of the "old man" as rubbish is quite normal for converts. The power of the conversion experience makes everything else seem irrelevant. This happens all the time in love affairs. In finding the right girl, all my previous loves seem like mere infatuations. We wonder how we could have ever loved that old girl who seems so ordinary now. Well, Christians are the same way with their old saviors. My old philosophy, work ethic, or religion is now "worldly" and some people even consider it demonic. This kind of attitude explains how open-minded atheists can become narrow-minded Christian fanatics. This also helps us to see why converted people often leave their old church. They feel that it didn't give them this grand experience, so it's dead and useless.

This narrow-mindeness of converted lovers is natural and good for a while. Newlyweds should go overboard about their spouse. We don't expect them to have a balanced relationship. However, as time goes by and the relationship becomes more secure, it's normal for the couple to renew old relationships. It's the same in our Christian life. We probably should get one-dimensional for a while. For example, after my conversion, I gave up my study of philosophy and Oriental religions because I somehow sensed that I wasn't yet strong enough to incorporate them into my Christianity. After a few years however, I started to read them again and, predictably, much of it seemed like rubbish.

What happens is that after conversion we still need a formation, simply to understand what to do with our new life. This formation after conversion will determine the depth and extent of our transformation in Christ. If our formation is narrow, God will have a very small space to work. It is here that the old religious and secular formation comes in. Many of the things we learned before our conversion really were true. It was the fact that we weren't converted that made it all seem like nonsense. So I discovered with great surprise that my old boring theology courses now made a lot of sense. The psychology, philosophy, and sociology always did make sense, and, in a lot of ways, they helped lead me to the Lord. Anyway, at this point, I recovered the treasure of Catholicism. It provided a language, form, and context for my conversion to grow. Otherwise I had all the makings of a narrow-minded fanatic (but for the grace of God).

Here we can start to understand the difference between the Catholic and Reformed tradition in recent times.

The Catholic tradition tends to produce a few spiritual giants. The evangelical tradition produces a lot of spiritual babies. We need babies but babies need to grow up and reproduce themselves if the Church is going to be real. We have to take the two truths together (Charles Simpson in *New Covenant*, Vol. II, Aug. 1972, pp. 10-14).

This is not completely true, but as a general statement on the last hundred years it conveys the message. Evangelical Protestants tended to emphasize conversion. However, once this happened there was little formation to help people to grow. It was easy to get into the Kingdom but hard to get further along. There was little emphasis on growth in prayer or the need for community, teaching, and service. Because of this, many denominations never developed a theology of social action, but got stuck in the God-and-me relationship.

Just about the opposite happened in contemporary Catholicism. People had a well-developed theology, moral code, and social ethic, yet somehow it seemed that conversion was taken for granted. So a relatively few people who persevered went beyond the formation to become transformed by God. But when they did, the breadth of these people's formation gave God the chance to make them into heroes of the faith.

Of course, the obvious conclusion is to get the best of both traditions together which is what I described earlier. This also happens to be the reason why we are writing such an extensive program. Transformed Christians need a formation broad enough to allow them to let God into every aspect of their lives. (Actually this is more of an outline.) This is also the reason why the books seem to get more Catholic as you go along. *Friendship with Jesus* is basic Christianity, and this volume is rather explicitly Catholic. Protestants are usually good at evangelism; Catholics are good at providing formation. This is why I've been fanatically quoting the documents of Vatican II. These documents are the authoritative description of Catholic formation for the contemporary Church.

So with all of this we need to draw some conclusions from this understanding of the Church as a formation for transformation and then describe some Christian attitudes toward the world.

FORMATION
1. Understanding of personal responsibility—structure should lead us to a choice to be open to God's transforming power.
2. We need to incorporate our old formation (religious and secular) into our new transformed life.

3. The depth and extent of our transformation is conditioned by the quality of our formation.
4. The institutional Church is to lead us to become transformed by the Spirit and then to help us grow in that transformation.
5. Christians should work in political and economic areas to provide the best possible formation for people.

ATTITUDES TOWARD THE WORLD
"You can fence yourselves in but you can't fence the world out" (Gandalf in Tolkien's *Lord of the Rings*).

We can celebrate the goodness of the world (Genesis 1) in Christ, "arranging all things with him, playing upon the earth, delighting in the sons of men" (*Constitution on the Church in the Modern World*, n. 57). Christians can integrate the valid insights of psychology, sociology, medicine, science, and politics into their Christian life. We need to listen to and learn from the "signs of the times" which are a kind of a revelation of God's will.

This means that the beauty of art and culture is something a Christian can rejoice in. Beauty opens us up to God; the works of Beethoven and Shakespeare are gifts to lead me closer to God. We can share with the world the truth and beauty we have in common.

Finally, brethren, whatever is true, whatever is honorable, whatever is just, whatever is pure, whatever is lovely, whatever is gracious, if there is anything worthy of praise, think about these things (Philippians 4:8—RSV).

NON-CHRISTIAN RELIGION
This dialogue with the world and its goodness is also dialogue with non-Christian religions. Catholics are called by the Church to the "task of fostering unity and love among men" and to give "primary consideration . . . to what human beings have in common and to what promotes fellowship among them" (*Decree on Non-Christian Religions*). There is no blanket condemnation of these religions or their people in the Vatican documents. The Church can learn from these other religions and in a sense be

called to holiness by them. The love and service of men like Mahatma Gandhi convicts Christians of their tepedity and challenges them to let Christ's light shine out all the more. Again, the Council calls us to look for the good in all things:

The Catholic Church rejects nothing which is true and holy in these religions. She looks with sincere respect upon those ways of conduct and of life, those rules and teachings, which, though differing in many particulars from what she holds and sets forth, *nevertheless often reflect a ray of that truth which enlightens all men.* Indeed she proclaims and must ever proclaim Christ "the way, the truth and the life" (John 14:6) in whom men find the *fullness* of religious life and in whom God has reconciled all things to Himself (2 Corinthians 4:18-19).

The Church therefore has this exhortation for her sons: prudently and lovingly through dialogue and collaboration with the followers of other religions, and in witness of Christian faith and life, *acknowledge, preserve and promote the spiritual and moral good found among these men as well as the values in their society and culture* (*Declaration on Non-Christian Religions*, n. 2; italics added).

These were times in the Church when other religions were considered to be the work of the devil and any contact with these people was felt to be a kind of contamination. Hand in hand with this was a rather simplistic idea of salvation which considered all non-Christians as damned. Here the Council reverses those misconceptions and calls all Christians to love their non-Christians brothers and to look for the truth that they have found of God. This is to say that the Holy Spirit is at work among all men to bring them to the fullness of graces in Jesus.

Nor is God Himself far distant from those who in shadows and mazes seek the unknown God, for it is He who gives to all men life and breath and every other gift (cf. Acts 17:25-28) and who as Savior wills that all men be saved (I Timothy 2:4).

Those can also attain to everlasting salvation who through no fault of their own do not know the Gospel of

Christ or His Church, yet sincerely seek God and, moved by grace, strive by their deeds to do His will as it is known to them through the dictates of conscience. Nor does Divine Providence deny the help necessary for salvation to those who, without blame on their part, have not yet arrived at one explicit knowledge of God, but who strive to live a good life thanks to His grace (*Constitution on the Church*, n. 16; italics added).

This wisdom of the Council comes from the security of trusting in the power of God. We don't have to condemn other religions as evil but can trust that God is at work among them. Because we know how good it is to know Jesus, we believe that men of other faiths will also accept Him once they can see Him clearly.

A CAUTION

On a practical level this whole question of openness to the world and other religions is a bit more complicated. In actuality there are many Christians who consider the world evil and other religions as demonic. Very often they are offended if other Christians have too much contact with these worldly elements. And if someone were to become interested in yoga or Buddhism they would really worry for that person's soul.

Well, they had the same kind of problem in the Corinthian church. Some Christians were offended that their brother Christians had been eating food that had been consecrated to idols of other religions (I Corinthians 8). Paul says there is nothing wrong in doing this because we know "that an idol stands for something that does not really exist; we know that there is only one God" (v. 4). He says that the people who are worried about this have a weak conscience (v. 7). But, out of love, the Christians with strong conscience are to defer to the Christians with a weak conscience. "Be careful, however, and do not let your *freedom of action* make those who are weak in the faith fall into sin" (v. 9). This is not a matter of doctrine but of sensitivity and love. The truth is that there is nothing wrong here, but we shouldn't inflict this on those who are weak in the faith. Therefore, our *actions* shouldn't scandalize our weaker brothers. Paul is saying to the mature Christians, "We know that this is not essential to the Christian life, so we can be tolerant of their fears. However if you try to coerce them into believing something they're not ready for, then you're not really that mature yourself."

This notion that the rigorists are "weak in the faith" has more practical implications. As I mentioned before, Christians probably should go through a honeymoon phase where they are one-dimensional and everything is spiritual. *A Christian shouldn't strain to be open to the world and other faiths before he is secure in his relationship with Jesus.* To do this would simply confuse the person because his Christian identity isn't formed yet. This would be like a newlywed spending lots of time with old friends to the detriment of his relationship with his wife. There is a very real danger here that a person's primary relationship will be weakened if he goes out before that relationship is secure.

Also Christians have had different experiences of other religions. Some people have been led to the Lord through their involvement with yoga, etc., and they feel very positive about these spiritual disciplines. Others have been confused and hurt by their involvement. They experienced other religions as a real barrier to Christianity. In very rare cases this might have been a demonic trap (so can capitalism, achievements, or motherhood). Very naturally they are reluctant to have any further contact with that religion.

Again we need sensitivity here to try to understand each person's background. This happened dramatically with a visiting priest, Fr. Benedict from Dusseldorf, Germany. He had had a very positive experience with yoga which had helped him physically and in his prayer life. He couldn't understand why some Christians were so hostile to this and would often end up in arguments about this. Then one day the Lord told him, in prophecy, to be a little more tolerant because "what is food for you can be poison to others."

STRATEGY FOR COMMUNITIES
(CHARISMATIC POLITICS)

The basic questions are: "How shall our particular community try to affect our particular part of the world?" "What do we do about the elements of society that we consider inadequate or un-Christian?" Answers to particular situations usually fall within three general kinds of response: (1) political action, (2) witness in adversity, and (3) contemplative withdrawal.

1. *Political Action.* There are many situations where Christians can work to change existing social structures. The most obvious example was the civil rights movement in the U.S. where Christians endured great persecution to win equal rights for minorities. People were arrested, beaten, and shot as a witness to change the evil of legalized prejudice. It is important to remember that this was not just a viable option for Christians but a moral responsibility to win a people's God-given rights. There are similar situations where Christians should be trying to eliminate evil in our social structures. Usually the direction of such massive political action has to be encouraged by the hierarchy. For example, the priorities on social action for the Holy Year are on the problem of world hunger and women's rights. Perhaps we won't be able to quickly change the widespread structure and customs that support these kinds of injustices. The least we can do is to alert people to their responsibility in these areas. Also in our local environment we can start to curb our wasteful life-styles and to eliminate all kinds of prejudice against women. This is not a nice option, but a Christian responsibility of justice.

2. *Witness in Adversity.* There are times when Christians cannot change the existing social structures. More often large-scale changes (slavery, hunger, women's rights) take a great deal of time to come about. This was the situation for the early Christians in the Roman Empire. They couldn't change their society directly, so the strategy became *revolution through submission in joy.* And it works. Slaves, wives and citizens were to submit to their legal authorities: "For this is God's will: He wants you to silence the ignorant talk of foolish men by the good things you do" (2 Peter 2:15), and "God will bless you for this if you endure the pain of undeserved sufferings because you are conscious of His will" (2 Peter 2:19—TEV). This is the basis of a Christian non-violent revolution. We cannot use the weapons of the world (power, intrigue, domination), for "those who live by the sword

will perish by the sword." For a Christian to use these weapons of the world is to end up being corrupted himself. Rather, Christians are to witness to Christ by enduring these evil situations with joy and peace. In that way people will have a concrete demonstration of the power of God. This is the most we can do. Fr. James Reese summarizes St. Peter's non-violent strategy in these words: "*Even if you win the rat race you're still a rat.*"

3. *Contemplative Withdrawal.* When things in society get so corrupt that Christians can no longer in conscience even live with them, then they should get out. These are the times when a Christian says, "This system is so evil that for me to continue to participate in it would only prolong something I consider morally bankrupt." This is when Christians go to the desert to become a light to the world. Christians have been doing this for a very long time. When they feel that it is no longer possible for them to be a Christian in the existing society then they should withdraw. This strategy was made very popular when hippies started dropping out of society in the 60's. The idea is basically the same—to create an alternate life-style to the society you consider to be inhuman. Some Christians are called to be a leaven to change the society. Others cannot in conscience do that. This not only describes some contemplative religious orders but also individuals and family communities who decide to leave to become a "light on a hilltop." Rosemary Haughton has just started such a community. She reminds us that when people feel called to do this, they do it in a *non-judgmental way.* They are not saying that Christians in the world are wrong but that they feel God calling them into the desert. You do not withdraw from society to get a better view to criticize and judge others. You withdraw to help create the kind of life that you believe God is calling you to live. You become a witness over against the society to remind people that a Christian life-style still works.

FLEXIBILITY

Communities are like persons. They have needs that must be met if they are to grow to wholeness, freedom, and love.

Each of us needs to be loved, to have time alone to pray for creative work, friendships, recreation, etc. All of these needs are real and beg for a balance or integration if we are to be whole. This integration is not simply a schedule which gives equal time to each aspect of your life (though schedules help). This integration is becoming a fully human person being led by God's Spirit. Sometimes I might need to spend lots of time in prayer at the expense of my recreation, for example. Other times I will need to be more open to the world and my prayer time may diminish. There is a rhythm and a flow to life which is not just my moodiness but the revelation of God's will to me. The structure of our Christian life is not fixed like a chart but organic and flexible. This is true because the structure of our life is not so much a predetermined order as a response to the person of Jesus as He loves us. There are essential elements that must be there but their arrangement depends on our present response to the Spirit. Like baking a cake, there are certain basic ingredients but there are many recipes.

In our community life we must be wary of canonizing a particular spiritual recipe when all we really know are the basic ingredients. What is community? Love, Eucharist, Contemplation, Service, Creativity, Friendship. To emphasize just one of these aspects all the time is something like a heresy, as G.K. Chesterton described it: to have part of the truth and think that it is all of the truth.

Yet, as human beings, we cannot have all of these aspects all the time. We have limits, and in the journey of faith we don't always get a clear picture of what to do next. What happens is that sometimes we tilt more to contemplation, other times more to service or to play. That is the Spirit working among us, giving us the right recipe at the right time. This is what prophecy does for our lives. We hear "the word of the Lord" not just in prayer meetings, but through the Church leadership, spiritual directors, friends, books, and art. The Spirit speaks to us what God thinks we should be emphasizing at a particular time. This prophetic word is spoken to our concrete needs and realities as human beings. So there are no available models for what each Christian should be doing at a particular time. Look at the variety of the saints as they followed the Lord. Our communities too will have that kind of vital diversity as we follow the whispering of the

Spirit among us. Sometimes we rest in prayer, other times we work and serve; then we turn to each other and learn friendship and how to have fun together. It's like a great, constantly changing dance to holiness for the wedding feast of Jesus and His Church.

Eventually our openness to the good things of the world must be acted upon to make it real. Again the goal of Christianity is not to be a one-dimensional person. As St. Irenaeus said, "The glory of God is man fully allve." Not only are we partners with God in renewing the earth, but this begins with renewing ourselves to develop all our potential. Not only do we say that sociology is O.K. but we take time to study it if that's what we like. The same applies to all the arts and sciences. For example, Agnes Sanford (a great Christian writer and healer) takes time regularly to act in amateur drama. She doesn't do this to convert people, but basically because she likes it. Also it helps her keep in touch with where people are.

This is also a psychologically healthy thing to do in maintaining a well-balanced life. I know there are times when I get sick of talking about Christianity. I start taking myself too seriously and all these other Christians seem absolutely morbid. At those times I have to get out of what has become for me a suffocating hothouse. I go out and talk to non-Christians, read psychology and science fiction, play golf, go to plays, all to help regain my perspective. And at these times God seems to work more through these worldly things than through prayer meetings.

In addition to this is the broader reason that perfecting my talents gives glory to God. Finding joy in doing the best I can in my work and study is a way of praising God. Developing our human potential is as much a work of God's Spirit as prophecy. This includes eliminating oppression in any form and building the kind of society where man's work wil be creative instead of alienating. If we read a book like Studs Terkel's *Working* we find that most Americans find their work dehumanizing and boring. Surely this can't be God's will. Probably the same thing applies to our recreation and relationships with each other which are governed by television and functional isolation. There are many things that Christians need to learn here. The vision of Karl Marx has a good deal of truth to it. And advances in psychology, communication techniques and sociology should help Christians to lead a more human and loving life.

CONCLUSION

Christians are a leaven to the world. Leaven does nothing by itself. It needs to be hidden in the dough to change things. Christians cannot remain to themselves and expect to change the world. Of course what happens then is that both the leaven and the dough are transformed into something new. Christians' involvement in the world will change Christians, hopefully for the better. In any case we can't hide from the world. We are in the world, and whether we admit it or not the world is affecting Christianity. To isolate ourselves is to deny Christianity the possibility of transforming the world. "You can fence yourselves in but you can't fence the world out."

The Church's witness of love is to transform society. Each one of us has a part in changing the world. And the most amazing thing is that we Christians have the power in Jesus to change the world.

Mindful of the Lord's saying: "By this will all men know that you are my disciples, if you have love for one another" (John 3:35), Christians cannot yearn for anything more ardently than to serve the men of the modern world ever more generously and effectively. Therefore, holding faithfully to the Gospel and benefiting from its resources, and united with every man who loves and preaches justice, *Christians have shouldered a gigantic task demanding fulfillment in this world.* Concerning this task they must give a reckoning to Him who will judge every man on the last day.

Not everyone who cries, "Lord, Lord," will enter into the Kingdom of heaven, but those who do the Father's will and take a strong grip on the work at hand. Now the Father wills that in all men we recognize Christ our brother and love Him effectively in word and deed. By thus giving witness to the truth, we will share with others the mystery of the heavenly Father's love. As a consequence, men throughout the world will be aroused to a lively hope—the gift of the Holy Spirit—that they will finally be caught up in the peace and utter happiness in that fatherland radiant with the splendor of the Lord. "Now, to Him who is able to accomplish all things in a measure far beyond what we ask or conceive, in keeping with the power that is at work in us, to Him be the glory in the Church and in Christ Jesus down through all the ages of time without end. Amen" (Ephesians 3:20-21) (*Constitution on the Church in the Modern World*, n. 93; italics added).

BIBLIOGRAPHY

RECOMMENDED READING:

Abbott, Walter M., S.J., Gen Ed., *The Documents of Vatican II*, America Press, 1966, 793 pp.
  It is absolutely essential for Catholics to hear this prophetic message of the Council and integrate it into their lives. Charismatic Catholics need the Council's openness and balance to provide an adequate formation for their religious experience. (Especially the documents on the Church, Revelation, The Church in the Modern World *and* Ecumenism*).*

Haughton, Rosemary, *The Transformation of Man*, Paulist Press, New York, 1967, 280 pp.
  This is definitely the most influential book in forming our understanding of Christian community. A really profound look at how transformation occurs in all the aspects of our life. A very human and holy work.

Merton, Thomas, *Contemplation in a World of Action*, Doubleday & Co., Inc., Garden City, New York, 1973.
  Excellent book on the formation of contemplative community and its relationship to the world. Expresses the renewed understanding of the structure, authority and individuality of the postconciliar Church.

Tolkien, J.R.R., *The Lord of the Rings*, Ballantine Books, New York, New York, 1965. (3 Volumes).
  An absolutely glorious fantasy that is worth reading just for

the fun of it. Personally it has helped me more than any other contemporary work to understand what the Christian life is all about. Implicit in the tale are Christian attitudes toward the world, power, authority, service, and dedication—not to mention that enjoying a great work of literature is also very Christian.

SUPPLEMENTARY READING:

Berger, Peter, *The Sacred Canopy*, Elements of a Sociological Theory of Religion, Doubleday & Co., Inc., Garden City, New York, 1967, 229 pp.

Good, clear description of the sociological dynamics of community and the religious identity. Helpful in understanding the role of structure and personal choice in forming community.

Delespesse, Max, *The Church Community, Leaven and Life-Style*, The Catholic Centre of St. Paul University, Ottawa, Canada, 1968, 99 pp.

A very challenging book based on the experience and insight of the creator of the "International Centre for Community Life." This is a very revolutionary yet very Catholic concept of community. Particularly relevant is Chapter 5, "The Church as Community and the World."

Merton, Thomas, *Conjectures of a Guilty Bystander*, Doubleday & Co., Inc., Garden City, New York, 1968, 360 pp.

This, more than any of Merton's works, grips me with a power I find hard to understand. It is a very forceful, yet informal, book of personal meditations on Christianity, politics, art, etc. A profound insight on contemporary issues that forces you to re-evaluate your Christian life.

by Joseph Lange

Commitment 5

In almost every teaching in this series we have found that Jesus, His teaching, and the living out of the Christian life demand decisions, choices, and commitments. The Father, the Son, and the Spirit offer themselves to us, and, respecting our freedom, await our choice to love them, to give ourselves in return. The making of the "new" man is the transformation of all that we are into Christ—thoughts, feelings, attitudes, life-style, values—as love compels, until we have put on the mind and heart of Christ. And so, gradually, we become holy, saints, bound together in love and fidelity to other saints in the Body of Christ, a light and leaven to the world.

Such a transformation is only possible because of the decision to pursue the mystery of a life in the Spirit through to the end. That is the meaning of commitment: a choice, made once-and-for-all, renewed again and again, to see through to the end whatever I commit myself to. In this case, I mean a life-commitment, the investment of my whole life as a response to God's gift of Himself to me in Jesus and the Spirit.

There are two commandments for Jesus: Love the Lord your God with your whole heart, your whole soul, your whole strength, your whole mind; and love your neighbor as I have loved you. These are expressions of total commitment, of the risk of all of oneself for the treasure of a new life in God. Jesus asks for everything we are and everything we have. In many other ways He leaves no doubt that half-hearted loving is simply not enough.

As they were making their way along, someone said to Him, "I will be Your follower wherever You go." Jesus said to him, "The foxes have lairs, the birds of the sky have nests but the Son of Man has nowhere to lay His head." To another He said, "Come after Me." The man replied, "Let me bury my father first." Jesus said to him, "Let the dead bury their dead; come away and proclaim the Kingdom of God." Yet another said to Him, "I will be Your follower, Lord, but first let me take leave of my people at home." Jesus answered him, "Whoever puts his hand to the plow but keeps looking back is unfit for the reign of God" (Luke 9:57-63).

On one occasion when a great crowd was with Him, He turned to them and said, "If anyone comes to Me without turning his back on his father and mother, his wife and children, his brothers and sisters, indeed his very self, he cannot be My follower. Anyone who does not take up his cross and follow Me cannot be My disciple" (Luke 14:25-27).

Jesus said to all: "Whoever wishes to be My follower must deny his very self, take up his cross each day, and follow in My steps. Whoever would save his life will lose it, and whoever loses his life for My sake will save it" (Luke 9:23-24).

The question which the Gospel puts to us is not how I fit Christ into my life, but how I fit my life into Christ. Each of us has his or her own feelings and attitudes and possessions and lifestyle. We find room in our lives for this person or that, this work or that. Our lives are more or less in ruts, comfortable and familiar ruts. Jesus asks for more than just a little time here or a minor adjustment there. He does not want to be fitted into our schedule somewhere. He wants us to adjust our whole lives to Him, to be made entirely new.

The other day a group of us were discussing the question: What does it feel like when you hear the unqualified call to total commitment? One of the men said, "Part of me acknowledges the truth of it and wants to respond, and part of me doesn't want to hear it." To which I replied, "And isn't it usually the case that at just that point we turn our attention elsewhere just so we don't have to think about it? Don't we always put off responding to that call for total response?" I believe that most of us do put off responding most of the time. We fit Christ into our lives instead of fitting our lives into Christ. That is why it is so important for us to look more closely at the need and nature of commitment.

One of the more common characteristics of youth since the 1960's is the delay of the choice of a life-direction. The studies I have seen indicate that more and more young people are even putting off marriage until their late twenties. At the same time, there are clear signs of aimlessness, meaninglessness, and lack of integration in their lives. There is a groping for an identity and for meaning. It all fits together because it is only the choice of a life-commitment that provides identity, integration, and meaning.

A clear and definite commitment, in one sense, narrows down my possibilities. That I choose to be writing right now means that I cannot do anything else. On the other hand, precisely because I have chosen to write settles a number of things for me. To begin with, it allows me to develop the possibilities of writing, which would not have happened otherwise. Another thing it does is create a whole set of values for me. Some things will help me to write and others will not, so things begin to take on the values of "desirable" and "undesirable." Finally, it teaches me something about fidelity, about the need to renew the choice again and again.

There are obviously a lot of choices that we make in a lifetime. All of them exclude other possibilities, all of them create values, and all of them are related to fidelity. The depth to which these choices transform us depends on how central the object of choice is to the person we are and can become. The ultimate choice is to risk our whole life by the commitment to a life-direction. The choice of living for myself or for God is the choice proclaimed by the Gospel. "Unless the seed falls into the ground and dies it shall not bear fruit." "He who would save his life will lose it."

In the choice to respond to the invitation of Jesus, we are called upon to risk our whole self. The choice to live for Jesus excludes any other life-style, any other living for myself. Now Jesus is my *only* Lord and my *only* Savior. It is His will I seek, and I no longer seek my own. I place *all* my trust in Him and *all* my hopes and *all* my dreams.

Also, because I choose Jesus as the very center of my life, I also choose a whole set of values. Everything ranges itself before me as that which will help or hinder me from drawing closer to Him. Everything begins to appear as consistent or inconsistent with my commitment to share myself with Him. I have taken on a new identity: one who loves Jesus and one who is loved by Jesus. Spending time with Him is worth doing. Being too busy to spend time with Him is inconsistent and undesirable. This, incidentally, is the reason that persecution for Jesus' sake is always inevitable for a true follower of Jesus. The values of Jesus stood as a judgment against pride and power, lying and unforgiveness, wasted and empty lives. When we choose Jesus and begin to take on His values, the judgment is felt by others simply because of our life-style. People don't like to feel judged, so they persecute and ridicule.

The point that needs to be appreciated here is that the choice to make a total commitment is not just desirable, it is a necessity, if there is to be direction, growth, integration and meaning in my life. Without commitment there is no direction, without commitment there are no values. Everything appears as equally desirable, and where everything is of equal value, nothing is of any value, including one's own life.

We are dealing here with one of the deepest aspects of what it is to be human: choosing life-directions, not because of temporary feelings, but out of our deepest freedom. Meaninglessness and aimlessness are the direct results of lack of commitment.

Superficial Christianity and cheap conversions which do not call clearly for total commitment do not produce transformed lives. Perhaps people begin to use a new language about Jesus and the Spirit, perhaps there is a rearrangement of a segment of their lives, but nothing is radically changed, as these "Christians" continue on with their same insensitivity to people, blindness to the needs of the poor, and all the bondage of the world and the flesh. Very often their guilt increases, instead of being relieved, because they have not made the commitment which makes the relief of their guilt possible. The failure to proclaim the call to total commitment is a betrayal of the Gospel and of the people to whom it is preached.

The integration of our lives, the sense that we are one with ourselves and within ourselves, one with God, and one with His

creation is only possible through total commitment. The integration of my personal past, present, and future is achieved as I
choose Jesus because I can see my past leading to my new life,
the present acting out of it, and the mystery of the future as all of
one piece.

Total commitment to anyone or anything can provide direc-
tions and integrations, of course, and examples abound. Men and
women have devoted themselves to medicine and science and art
and to marriage partners. A level of wholeness and happiness
results. These people and things have become saviors. The commitment to Jesus offers the ultimate wholeness and meaning and
integration because it means a full life shared with Jesus and the
Father in the power of the Spirit, the promise of eternal life, and
a share in the work of establishing God's reign with one's own
life. Jesus alone is the Way, since only in Him is all wholeness
achieved. Only through Him can we become the magnificent person He created each of us to be. Only in our mutual total commitment to Him and to each other can all of mankind be brought
together in the love and harmony He wants for us.

So, total commitment to Jesus is not just desirable, it is necessary. The question, then, the task, becomes one of fidelity,
where fidelity is not just a matter of rigidly keeping a promise,
but an openness to growth. Fidelity is worked out as the continued affirmation of the choice once made as the implications of
the choice play themselves out in our day-to-day lives. All of this
was worked out in many ways through the first three volumes of
this series.

Another essential dimension of our total commitment to
Jesus is the inclusion of our commitment to the Body of Christ,
the Church. We have already worked out the scriptural base for
that, and some of its implications. Now we want to look at some
of the practical forms that we might take.

COMMITMENT TO THE
LOCAL CHURCH OR PARISH

We are not going to grow together into the Messianic Presence unless we are committed together to do that in a specific
group in a specific place. For most of us that will be our local

church. Today, as always, local churches vary in the quality of commitment of both leader and people, so there is no single model or formula for what to do. It is really unrealistic to expect that perfection will be found anywhere, so the current state of the local church is not so much a matter to be deplored as welcomed. The attitude of welcome can only come from a sense of what the Lord is about right now in His people. He is showing mercy to us. He is calling *us* forth, and hundreds of thousands of others, to be the leaven and light to His people. That is really good, and especially good to keep in mind. Let's not be frustrated about the way things are. Let's recognize that we have turned the corner and the Lord is doing something.

To get practical, let me begin by reviewing some of the things we should not do, and discuss some ways of dealing with the frustrations of where we are.

First of all, we should not consider ourselves to be the saviors of the Church. Aside from being wrong, and aside from creating impossible burdens for us, it readily communicates to others a sense of our own self-importance and self-righteousness, which alienates them and prevents us from achieving what we are about in the first place, which is to help them to a deeper relationship with Jesus.

The behavior patterns which grow out of the "Savior" attitude include things such as going to the pastor and telling him that he needs the baptism of the Spirit, standing up in church on Sunday and speaking or emoting during Mass, judging all the officers and parishioners and speaking negatively of them, etc.

We have got to understand and be convinced in our hearts that conversion, baptism of the Spirit, and certain forms of worship, such as prayer meetings, do not make us holy. They are only the beginning of a new life. The people we meet in our neighborhoods and churches may very well be holier than we are—many of them are. If we are so blinded by our experience of the Spirit that we do not look for the good in others, then we will never do them or the Lord any good.

So, we must begin with the truth about ourselves, that we are in part just beginners and sinners. We must learn patience and real love that does not condemn but saves. We must not run ahead of the Lord in our service but, having asked to be used, wait for Him to show us how and when.

I once met a man who had moved to a small town with his family about a year before. There were three Masses on Sunday morning at the Catholic church there. He began to go to all three, arriving early and staying late, in order to get to know the parishioners. He volunteered his services whenever there was a need, and he worked at anything which needed to be done. He did not preach or talk about the Lord. He just served with an obvious cheerfulness that came from a love without designs. He was content to love and serve and leave the results up to the Lord. After about six months a few people began to ask him about his peace and cheerfulness. Then he was able to tell them about Jesus and the Spirit. Today there is a flourishing Charismatic *and* parish Renewal there.

We all share in Christ's authority to love, to speak the truth in love, to announce the Kingdom, and to lay down our lives for our brothers and sisters. To truly exercise the authority of Jesus we must do as Jesus did: say nothing and do nothing except what the Father wills. There are lots of good things to do, but what and when are matters of discernment, and that discernment ought to be tested. I am convinced that lots of times, most of the time, the Father does not want us to preach, but to serve silently in love.

We are talking about total commitment to the life of the Church and the parish, the local Body of Christ. That commitment is worked out, not by self-serving attempts to change others into our image of what they should be, but by simple, loving service of their needs. I know clergy and people everywhere who are being turned off by "Christians" who are always talking and never doing anything.

Another thing to avoid is being willing to do only "significant" work in the parish. The life of the Body has many needs. The place to begin to serve is where the needs are right now. As you love these without strings, you become a source of change.

We also need to beware of the changes in language that we might pick up from an ecumenical environment. God knows I praise Him constantly for what He is doing to bring His people together. But if we start talking a whole new religious language to our fellow Catholics (Presbyterian or Lutheran, etc.), they will not understand us, and a wall has been erected between us. We desperately need to think through and learn to describe our experience in the language of our own traditions. This creates depth, a new appreciation of our own traditions, and a means of communicating to those within our traditions.

Once we have come to terms with the deep selfishness of our own impatience and the desire to change everyone to our liking right now, then we can begin to be fruitful for the Lord with peace and patience and love.

An important place to start is prayer. The deeper and richer our prayer life and the closer we get to the Lord, the more clearly the Spirit will shine through us and work through us. I once heard a Baptist minister describe the remarkable change in his church over a couple of years from the time one woman came daily to the church to pray for it. Our intercessory prayer is extremely important.

Agnes Sanford describes how she and a small group of her friends made a point of getting to her church fifteen minutes before the service to pray for the healing of all the parishioners and for the Spirit to work powerfully that Sunday. They prayed *secretly*. She emphasized that. And usually they picked out people who came to church that morning who looked hurting in some way and prayed especially for them. She reports that the Church became a really peaceful and loving place in a couple of years, so that one could hardly go in there without feeling God's presence.

Another thing to do is simply love the people of your church. Look around your neighborhood for the lonely, the hurting. Look around your church on Sunday for those who are alone. Invite them to breakfast. Make friends. Build up the Body by putting yourself on the line. When I think of what could happen if everyone now being touched by God's Spirit would begin to take a personal interest in one or two lonely people in the neighborhood or parish, I really get excited. Speaking in tongues is good, but without love it is like tinkling cymbals and sounding brass.

Finally, by no means look upon a prayer group as a community. In the old days we had novena devotions, benediction, block rosaries, and things like that as devotional aids. That is what a prayer meeting is for. Your community is your Church, and only to the extent that it leads you into deeper love and actual involvement in your Church will it be of lasting value to you and renewing for your Church. We will know that our prayer meetings are healthy when we regularly get witnesses in them of the ways the Lord is using us in our churches.

The community to which most of us are called is the local church. Service commitments to politics, social work, or diocesan involvement are essential to the work of the Church too, as was pointed out in the last chapter. Such commitments can be very fruitful, but their real power develops not from an isolated presence, but from a community presence. In that context there is all the life-sharing that reveals the love of Christ among us. It is both the most fruitful environment for growth and the most effective witness of the power of the Spirit.

It is an exciting thing to watch schools and social agencies and officers of education being transformed by the building of faith communities. All over the country today such transformations are taking place. People are praying together at work, loving each other, and loving the people they serve. Praise God!

THE RELIGIOUS LIFE

Another form of community to which the Lord may be calling some is the religious life as a sister, priest, brother or monk. In former times we used to have a special reverence for religious. They were the "holy" ones, we thought. It was one of the unfortunate aspects of the Catholic culture that was never true but was taken as true by the popular mentality. That error is being corrected in many ways, not the least of which are the lay movements of spirituality from which the religious are learning.

The calling to serve the Lord in a religious community is a special call to a special form of community life. That life is not better; it is just different from the call to serve in the community of the parish. There are hundreds of religious communities to choose from, each with its own family spirit and tradition. From their beginnings they have enriched the Church by their example of communal life and service in almost every area of human need.

For those who feel called to the religious life, methods of testing this leading of the Spirit have evolved over the centuries. Each community differs, but the requirements usually include letters of recommendation, a period of living with the community without obligations for a time, and finally the discernment of the formation personnel.

If you feel the Spirit leading you to any of these communities, it is a good first step to talk it over with your spiritual director. A good second step is to discuss it with your diocesan director of vocations.

Another option today is one of the new forms of communal life the Spirit is raising up in a few places around the country. The charismatic renewal has been the spawning ground of a few covenant communities, of groups of people who feel led to share their lives by commitment to a form of community life different from the current forms of religious life. These groups, too, have their own family spirit and distinctive life-styles.

It might be helpful to describe something of our community as an example of this new style. You have already encountered our teaching program in these four volumes. Along the way you have been exposed to most of the principles and the flavor of our life together. Founded in 1970, we currently number only eighty to ninety people from the ages of about eighteen to seventy. Our people come from all kinds of backgrounds and are involved in all sorts of employment. Father Bob Devine, O.S.F.S., and I are the directors of the community. We have a staff of six that meets weekly to pray together and to take care of the nitty-gritty of daily administration. We have a pastoral team of thirteen that meets every two weeks to talk over what the Lord is doing among us and to attempt to discern His will for us.

We have about thirty teachers; a teacher training program; a communication skills workshop; six different kinds of retreats, with one or another given every other week; a formation team whose job is to see to the personal attention of anyone who is going through our teaching programs; a secretarial staff; a music team; a coffee house team; a newsletter; a bookstore; a tape library; and other offices that serve the life and work of the community. We have recently begun to develop a farm that was given to us and an arts and crafts program.

Some of our people work in the diocese as religious education coordinators, some in the social services of Catholic Charities, and some at the diocesan retreat center.

We have gone individually or sent teams in response to invitations to give workshops, retreats, and conferences to Protestants and Catholics in about twenty states. It has been really exciting to share the Lord's love with hundreds of Protestant ministers and their people, with bishops, with close to a thousand priests and seminarians, with about two thousand sisters and about twenty thousand laity.

We have studiously avoided developing monastic structures and practices. Our community is for people from all walks of life, and we feel that the Lord wants us to provide a life-style that is as unstructured as possible. Our main concerns are loving God and our neighbor, the call to freedom and personal responsibility, openness to all God is doing in His church and between the churches, and coming to wholeness (salvation) in the fullness of our uniqueness and relatedness. So, we have no households, no talk of headship and submission, but only the demands of love in personal response-ability.

If all this sounds like blowing our own horn, it is not intended to. It is only a sharing of what God is doing among us, and I think it is important to say that it works. We have enjoyed the Lord and continue to marvel at the way He is setting us free.

Finally, the whole point of this chapter is that we need to be committed people. God is committed to us. The total commitment He calls us to involves the life-determining choice to be His and our neighbor's in the concrete context of a specific community. We cannot afford to put off making and living out that commitment.

BIBLIOGRAPHY

RECOMMENDED READING:

O'Connor, Elizabeth, *Call to Commitment*, Harper and Row, New York, New York, 1963, 205 pp.
    A delightfully readable book about the Church of the Savior in Washington, D.C. Solid teaching and challenging.

Postscript

Provisions for the Pilgrimage

One definite characteristic of pilgrims is that they are a restless people. They don't carve out a niche and get comfortable. They keep on moving. And no matter how good and exciting the journey is, pilgrims know that it only makes sense if they reach their goal.

We are all pilgrims, God's restless people always hungering for more of Jesus. This is the mystery. There is always more to discover. There is always more of Jesus. And so we keep on moving deeper into the mystery or we die. Like the mustard seed, it's always that choice: either grow or die.

What we have described in these four volumes is just the beginning of the journey. *Living Christian Community* is only an outline or guidebook for the pilgrimage. Perhaps that might depress you. But if you've tasted the excitement of living with Jesus, this should bring the joy of knowing that there is so much more to taste and enjoy. This isn't some pie-in-the-sky optimism. It is our experience. By walking the journey of faith, the new Exodus is "heaven all the way to Heaven" (Fr. Richard Rohr's tape on the "Exodus," *St. Anthony's Messenger*).

WHERE DO WE GO FROM HERE?

What I want to do now is to point out some further opportunities for growth in addition to our bibliographies. Some of these are within a charismatic context but most of them are from the broader life of the Church.

153

1. *Community Life.* Taking to heart Jesus' advice "to build on rock," I think we should first of all look to the kind of communities that have endured throughout the centuries. After all, it takes a good bit of time to discern what will last like rock. In the Catholic Church this endurance in faith is most readily found in the larger religious orders. Studying the history of these orders and experiencing their present community life will teach us a great deal about the dynamics of community.

● *Focolare Movement*—This community-based movement has grown and maintained its enthusiasm since its founding in World War II. More than any other contemporary group we were impressed by the Focolares' love, service, and life style.

● *Catholic Worker Movement*—The Charismatic Renewal especially needs to assimilate this witness of service to the poor.

● *Contemporary Communities*—Prayer groups in Providence, New Orleans, Houston and Ann Arbor and many other places have developed different charismatic styles of community. Each one has strengths and weaknesses that help us discover what to embrace and what to avoid in our own communities. Regardless of style, to visit one of these is to encounter the power and presence of Jesus in His people.

2. *Movements.* Cursillo, Marriage Encounter, and Movement for a Better World are all renewal movements geared to a particular aspect of the Christian life. While they do not attempt a full community life, they still have many strengths to incorporate into community. As for *social action*, aside from local programs and governmental activities, some areas deserve particular mention. The Farm Workers Boycott is still a way to participate in winning rights for the underprivileged. A good comprehensive plan for Christian political involvement is *Bread for the World.*

3. *Adult Education.* Some ideas are:
   ● Serendipity Program by Lyman Coleman
   ● Faith at Work Conferences
   ● Masters program in Applied Spirituality with Fr. Donald Gelpi—University of San Francisco
   ● Houses of Prayer—retreats and teaching programs
      The best known are Madonna House, Cambremere, Canada, and H.O.P.E., Convent Station, New Jersey.

- Tapes—especially good series on Scripture is by Fr. Richard Rohr (St. Anthony's Messenger Service) and "The New Testament for Today" (Alba House Communications)
- Contact local colleges and diocesan offices of education for theology courses, communication skills and pastoral counseling workshops, etc.

In listing all of these resources, I don't want to give the impression that the Christian life is a matter of scholarship on different spiritualities. Christianity is not so much a matter of learning but a life of loving. Our study links us up with the treasures of the Catholic tradition. It gives us a sense of balance and new insights to grow deeper in the Lord. However, most of the battle is won "in the trenches," so to speak. It is our faithfulness in those everyday choices to love that really make the difference. Real growth comes in our being open to Jesus every day in prayer. It is as unspectacular as our little acts of love and service for our fellow Christians. Of course, there will be great breakthroughs and marvelous spiritual experiences, but, as always, we know that "without love I am nothing."

Perhaps the best provision for the pilgrimage is to develop an attitude of longing for Jesus, to hunger for love. St. Paul describes it best.

All I want is to know Christ and the power of His resurrection and to share His sufferings by reproducing the pattern of His death. That is the way I can hope to take my place in the resurrection of the dead. Not that I have become perfect yet; I have not yet won, but I am still running trying to capture the prize for which Christ Jesus captured me. I can assure my brothers, I am far from thinking that I have already won. All I can say is that I forget the past and *I strain ahead for what is still to come; I am racing for the finish*, for the prize to which God calls us upward to receive in Christ Jesus. . . . If there is some point on which you see things differently, God will make it clear to you; meanwhile, let us go forward on the road that has brought us to where we are (Philippians 3:10-16—JB).

Appendix
Order in Marriage and the Role of Women in the Church

Since in our time women have an ever more active share in the whole life of society, it is very important that they participate more widely also in the various fields of the Church's apostolate (*Decree on the Apostolate of the Laity*, n. 9).

We also urge that women should have their own share of responsibility and participation in the community life of society and likewise of the Church (The Synod of Bishops, 1971, as quoted in *Vatican Study Commission on Women in Society and in the Church*, p. 24).

This section was originally part of the chapter on marriage. Since it is such a controversial topic we thought it best to save it for a fuller treatment as an appendix. The whole topic is primarily a matter of scriptural interpretation, especially in regard to St. Paul's statements on Christian marriage. This in turn affects how we see women's role in the Church. What I basically want to do is to analyze the sections in Scripture on order in marriage, relying heavily on Church documents for the interpretation. Then I want to describe a few practical consequences for our daily lives.

ROLE OF WOMEN IN SCRIPTURE

It is clear that the Old Testament concept of women is in many ways identical to other societies of that time period.

157

Woman is subordinate to man in all aspects of social life. She is his property (Genesis 12:12-20; 20:2, 9; 19:8; Exodus 20:17). Yet women occupied a relatively high position in the Jewish religion. Especially in the stories of Ruth, Esther, Deborah and Judith, we see women of heroism, intelligence, and a clear and often decisive vocation from God for the Jewish community. What is most important for us to remember is that in the creation narrative woman is described as being equal to man.

God created man in his image,
in the divine image he created him;
male and female he created them (Genesis 1:22).

When man first sees woman he exclaims: "This at last is bones of my bones and flesh of my flesh." This means that for him (man) she was like another self.

It is only after the fall that woman's role is seen as submissive to man. This submission is clearly the result of sin. It is part of the curse that:

Your urge shall be for your husband,
And he shall be your master (Genesis 2:16).

Therefore female submission, like sickness, hatred, and death, is not part of God's perfect will for us; rather it is seen as one of the effects of man's sin.

Because of sin, the order willed by God is seriously disturbed. Woman's love for her husband is degraded, becoming lust and seduction; henceforth man will act as dominant over woman. Redemption will come only in Christ. He will bring liberation which will restore the original balance of God's work (*International Women's Year 1975: Vatican Study Commission on Women in Society and in the Church*, p. 12).

In the Gospels, Jesus' teaching and actions show a clear break with the Old Testament idea of the inferiority of women. His teaching on the indissolubility of marriage (Mark 10:6-11) establishes women's equal rights, whereas in the Old Testament a woman could be divorced by her husband and had no legal rights.

Jesus' parables also describe God in parallel images of male and female (Matthew 13:33; 25:1; Luke 15:8; 18:1). For example, in a *male* parable, God, the shepherd, searches out the lost sheep. This is immediately paralleled with God, the woman, finding the lost coin (Luke 15:4-10).

As the Vatican Study on the International Women's Year points out:

> Jesus had no hesitancy in refusing to reduce woman to her functional role of mother. When the woman exclaimed "Blessed is the womb that bore You and the breasts that gave You suck," He replied, "Happy rather are those who hear the word of God and keep it" (Luke 11:27-28) (p. 20).

Jesus' actions even more clearly demonstrate woman's equality. He reveals himself as Messiah to the Samaritan woman at the well. In the very act of talking to a woman in a public place, He shocked the Apostles—not to mention that a Samaritan woman was considered by the Jews to be perpetually under a menstrual taboo. Here Jesus clearly breaks with the religious and sexual prejudices that supported a male-dominant society. He accepts Mary as a disciple (Luke 10:40) and after his Resurrection He appears first to Mary Magdalene and gives her the task of being the first witness (John 21).

In her book *What a Modern Catholic Believes about Women* (Thomas More Press, Chicago, Ill, 1972), Sr. McGrath points out that the importance of this commission has often been rationalized away, as in a 1930's Episcopal report on the ministry of women in which it was stated: "The appearance to St. Mary Magdalene was not reckoned among the appearances which may be termed official, on which the belief of Christendom was to rest" (p. 23). Sr. McGrath adds: "Apparently Christ did not understand the difference between His official and unofficial appearances" (p. 23).

For the Jews, women were legal minors, and their testimony was not considered official. Thus the post-Resurrection appearance emphasizes that Jesus considered Mary as responsible a witness as the Apostles. In the Apostolic Church women were full members with the men. After the Ascension, "they gathered together frequently to pray as a group, together with the women and with Mary the Mother of Jesus" (Acts 1:14—TEV). They prophesied, taught and served as deaconesses in the community (Acts 6:1; 9:36ff; 12:12; 16:13ff; 17:12, 34). Priscilla shared the office of teaching with her husband Aquila, and twice Paul mentions her before her husband which was certainly not the custom of the time (Acts 18:26; 2 Timothy 4:14). Also, she is once described as joining with her husband to correct another teacher's doctrine—a man named Apollos (Acts 18:26).

However, in regard to marriage, it is clear that the writers of the epistles advocate male authority and female submission—e.g., "Wives should be submissive to their husbands as to the Lord" (Ephesians 5:22; also cf. 1 Corinthians 11:3; 7:10; 14:35; Colossians 3:18). Here St. Paul bases his theological argument on Chapter 2 of Genesis. The man is superior to the wife because he was created first. However, the first creation account has man and woman clearly created as equals. And the second account does not deal with the history of creation so much as to answer the questions: Why sin? Why marriage? Why are things the way they are?

In the teachings of Paul there is a tension between practical guidelines and universal Christian principles. Slaves, women, children and citizens are to be submissive to appointed authorities. This was an accommodation to the existing social structure. There were no provisions for changing these structures, since the Christians had no political power. Also, the good order of the Roman Empire helped the growth of Christianity.

Within the Christian community, however, the relationships were somewhat different. "Slaves are free in the Lord" and "Masters are slaves to the Lord" and all relationships are to be governed by love:

> Let all parties think humbly of others as superior to themselves, each of you looking to others' interests rather than to your own (Philippians 2:3).

In the Lord there are no distinctions between the members of a Christian community. The universal principle is equality in God's love.

There does not exist among you Jew or Greek, slave or freeman, male and female. *All are one in Christ Jesus* (Galatians 3:28)

The Vatican Study Commission sees this passage as a vision of a radically different approach to men and women. It notes that Paul uses the phrase "male and female" in the same way as Chapter 2 of Genesis, thus emphasizing that through Jesus there is a new creation.

In the new creation (Galatians 6:15) the duality of the sexes is assumed into the unity of the new man. All are one in Christ. All Christians have the same fundamental vocation, i.e., to become children of God by faith, to become ever more conformed to the image of the Son of God (Romans 8:29).

So we are faced with a dilemma. How can Paul urge women to be submissive to the husband if "all are one in Christ"? This is part of the much broader dilemma of distinguishing, in Scripture, practical guidelines from universal truths for all men for all times. The Vatican document points out that the Church has to discern revelation from what is merely an inspired response. For example, why don't we follow the dietary laws in the Acts of the Apostles? Why is the Eucharist a sacrament and not the washing of the feet? Jesus tells us to do both. Why don't we all sell our possessions like the early Jerusalem community? Why don't we accept slavery as a normal aspect of society? The reason is that the Spirit leads the Church to discern what is the revealed essence of the Scriptures. St. Paul himself does this when he insists that the Jewish practices of some of the converts are not part of Jesus' revelation of the Law. God wants us to live in the New Covenant. People may follow these codes if they wish, but they will not bring salvation, and are not necessary for all Christians. So the basic question is: "Are St. Paul's guidelines on order in marriage revealed universal laws for all Christians for all times?"

To answer this, the first point is that Paul's teaching on marriage is in the part of his letters entitled "household codes." (An exception is 1 Corinthians, where Paul responds to specific questions.) Female submission to male authority is placed alongside a whole hierarchy of obedience, including the submission of slaves, children and citizens. These household codes were prevalent social norms in first-century Rome. They are stoic virtues, and similar lists can be found in Epictetus and Seneca.

As far as these household codes being normative for all Christians, we have already seen a considerable change in the Church's discernment of God's will in these situations. For example, it wasn't until the twelfth century that slaves were recognized as having the right to marry. And it wasn't until the nineteenth century that slavery was widely recognized as something contrary to the Gospel. The Spirit guiding the Church has given us a different understanding of what kind of social structures are Christian. I doubt if any would promote the restoration of slavery in order to be literally faithful to the Bible. And since the Nuremberg trials, Watergate, widespread corruption in dictatorships, and the abortion movement, we cannot take it for granted that "the ruler (civil authority) is God's servant to work for your good" (Romans 13:4). In fact there is a rather strong theology regarding the occasions when civil disobedience is a Christian responsibility.

The point is that the Church has understood these household codes to be subject to change as the Spirit gives us an understanding of social structures which are more human and Christian. Second, even in Genesis we have male hegemony/female submissiveness presented as a *result of sinfulness.* Therefore becoming a "new creation" in Jesus should overcome the barriers and effects of sinfulness so that "all are one in Christ Jesus" (Galatians 3:28). Third, *it is interesting that the documents of Vatican II never even mention headship or submission in regard to marriage.* This does not mean that the Council thinks it is wrong, but rather that it was not important enough to mention in a relatively brief article. The Council did say things such as: "Christian husbands and wives are cooperators in grace" and "It (marriage) needs the kindly communion of minds and joint deliberation of spouses." If not the letter, then at least the spirit of the Council indicates something broader than male headship. And if male headship were the revealed core of what Christian marriage is about, I would certainly have expected the headship of the Church to have discerned this explicitly.

To summarize this section in Paul's teachings on marriage I want to refer again to the Vatican Study Commission on the International Women's Year:

> Compared with the Gospel, the teaching on marriage by Paul seem somewhat severe. Paul asks wives to be subject to their husbands, "for the husband is the head of the wife" (Ephesians 5:27), but he first proclaims the general principle: "Be subject to one another out of reverence for Christ" (Ephesians 5:21). In 1 Corinthians 7:3-4 he declares emphatically that wife and husband are equal in the exercise of conjugal rights. And he recognizes the right of women to pray and prophesy in the assembly held for worship, ordering them to keep their heads covered (1 Corinthians 11:2-16). Present exegesis interprets this "veil" of the woman in prayer more and more as a sign of her autonomy with respect to men when she addresses God. Some texts, it is true, impose "silence on women in the assembly" (1 Corinthians 14:34-35; 2:11-15). But these different disciplinary measures, and other similar prescriptions, were partially inspired by the Jewish notion of the time and should not be considered normative for subsequent periods (p. 16).

In the same vein, Fr. John McKenzie, S.J., probably the dean of American Catholic Scripture scholars, resolves Paul's apparent contradiction between the universal teaching of Christian equality and the household codes of male headship and female submission:

> The apparent antinomy probably arises because Paul, conditioned by the customs of the society in which he lived, saw in the emancipation of woman in the Roman world a breakdown of genuine morality. Rather than surrender to the general relaxed morals, Christians should maintain what to Paul was the traditional and solid basis of Jewish family life, even though he knew the subjection of women was the result of a curse. With the removal of the curse of sin, the subjection also should be removed but not by a sudden upheaval of soci-

ety. The principle is established, and as men and women grow in the life of regeneration, woman also will recover the position which is rightly hers by nature, and lost by sin (*Dictionary of the Bible*, Bruce Publishing Co., Milwaukee, Wis., 1965, p. 954).

St. Paul's teaching on male headship is an inspired pastoral teaching on how first-century Christians could integrate their Christianity with the popular culture. It is not a universal teaching which applies to all Christians of all times. As Edward Schillebeeckx describes it, male headship is simply a matter of "pastoral guidance within a definite historical setting" (*Marriage, op. cit.*, p. 200). It is an inspired teaching but is *not revelation* in the sense that the Eucharist, love or forgiveness would be a revelation of God's nature and the way He wants us to live. The revealed core of Christian marriage is that husband and wife should love one another as "Christ loved the Church and gave his life for it" (Ephesians 5:25—TEV). Love is essential. This love can be expressed in a variety of life-styles of which male headship is only one possibility. I am not saying that a Christian cannot choose this style of marriage. What I am saying is that it is a matter of discernment for each couple to decide which marital life-style the Lord wants for them.

In our community teaching about marriage we do not use the language of headship and submission because we think that it is an inadequate way to talk about two people loving each other. In other cultures in the past people had a concrete experience of loving relationships of authority and submission. This is very rare in our democratic society. When people hear the word "submission" they immediately have a feeling of inferiority and subservience. The result is that the people who teach about female submission have to spend a lot of time trying to contradict the normal meaning of submissiveness as inferiority.

What we have found is that married people need to learn how to love, communicate and work through conflicts so that they will be united in following the Lord's will. This is a similar yet more intense description of how we Christians should relate to one another in community. This can and does happen in a headship structure. However, we feel that this structure is inadequate to meet the needs of modern Christians. We do have marriages where a form of male headship is exercised and that is a real witness of God's power. Most of the time, though, in marriage and community, we talk more about love and communication and the result has been that both the marriages and the community show a remarkably authentic love and understanding that one visiting leader could only call "communal contemplation." I don't wish to boast; I only want to say that it really works.

ROLE OF WOMEN IN THE CHURCH

The next question is, "Can women hold positions of responsibility in our communities and in the Church?"

In the Apostolic Church we have a mixed picture of women's role in the Church. Paul recognizes certain deaconnesses as helpful in spreading the Gospel and Priscilla was definitely a teacher. Yet later on he writes some personal advice to Timothy, "I do not allow women to teach or to have authority over men; they must keep quiet" (1 Timothy 2:12—TEV).

Over the years Paul's advice to Timothy has been the prevailing teaching and practice of the Catholic Church. I suppose you could say that there was a great deal of prejudice also. This is regrettable, yet there was a great deal of anti-feminine prejudice in all of society. In one sense there is a need for repentance of the attitudes that made women a second-class Christian for so long. Alongside of this we can also see that the Church has in many ways elevated the role of women and that the present movement for female equality is largely due to the Christian ideals that shaped Western culture.

To focus on the positive side of our tradition, we can see examples of women exercising authority with Church approval. First of all there were abbesses of large convents and religious orders who had ecclesial authority similar to bishops. They approved appointments to their area, and besides the normal running of an organization they had the authority to approve or deny to priests the faculties of hearing confession and preaching. We also have examples of women teachers, especially the great saints in the mystical tradition—Teresa of Avila, Catherine of Siena,

Called to Service

Julia of Norwich and Theresa of Lisieux. There is even an occasion where Catherine of Siena publicly rebuked the Pope and the Pope followed her advice. More importantly the Church has discerned that Teresa of Avila and Catherine of Siena are Doctors of the Church. This means that they are officially teachers for the whole Church, and that is a quite a way from Paul's advice that women not be allowed to teach.

Lastly we have the Church recognizing the civil and occasionally ecclesial authority of queens and other female rulers. Of course this feminine authority was due to a particular social structure and understanding of God's will, but the same logic can also be applied to our contemporary social structure where women are held to be competent in exercising political authority.

Finally we find in the Church honoring Mary the Mother of God a tradition and example for the equality and dignity of women of the Church. Pope Paul VI's recent exhortation *Marialis Cultis* (Feb. 2, 1974) describes how Mary is a model for modern women. First of all he recognizes a need for a renewal of the devotion to Mary to speak to a modern culture.

The picture of the Blessed Virgin presented in certain types of devotional literature cannot easily be reconciled with today's life-style, especially the way women live today. *In the home, woman's equality and co-responsibility are being justly recognized by laws and the evolution of customs* (p. 34).

First, the Virgin Mary has always been proposed to the faithful by the Church as an example to be imitated, not precisely in the type of life she led, and much less for the socio-cultural background in which she lived and which today scarcely exists anywhere. She is held up as an example to the faithful rather for the way in which, in her own particular life, she fully and responsibly accepted the will of God (cf. Luke 1:38), because she heard the Word of God and acted on it and because charity and a spirit of service were the driving force of her actions" (pp. 22-23).

The reading of the Scriptures, carried out under the guidance of the Holy Spirit, and with the discoveries of the human

166

sciences and the different situations in the world today being taken into account, will help us to see how Mary can be considered a mirror of the expectations of the men and women of our time. Thus, the modern woman, anxious to participate with decision-making power in the affairs of the community, will contemplate with joy Mary who, taken into dialogue with God, gives her active and responsible consent, not to the solution of a contingent problem, but to that "event of world importance," as the Incarnation has been rightly called (p. 16).

The modern woman will note with pleasant surprise that Mary of Nazareth, while completely devoted to the will of God, was far from being a timidly submissive woman or one whose piety was repellent to others; on the contrary, she was a woman who did not hesitate to proclaim that God vindicates the humble and the oppressed and removes the powerful people of this world from their privileged positions (Luke 1:51-53) (p. 19).

The situation we have in the Church is one where women are being welcomed and challenged to participate fully in the Church's life. At present the only form of leadership denied women is ordination to the priesthood. The Pope's teaching on this is that the Church in this regard is conditioned by the fact that the priest represents Jesus in his Incarnation as a man. Other than this, women are considered competent in all areas of teaching and pastoral responsibility. This is simply to recognize the fact that for years women have responsibly led religious orders of thousands of nuns, run schools, hospitals and colleges, and in many ways been in the vanguard of social work and the renewal of spirituality and theology (Mother Theresa, Dorothy Day, Rosemary Haughton and Chiara Lubich of the Focolare Movement, to name a few). In terms of lay association (Charismatic Renewal, Cursillo, etc.) there is absolutely no reason in Scripture or Church teaching why women cannot hold positions of leadership for prayer groups and communities. In fact, because the

Charismatic Renewal is predominantly female it would make sense to have an equal representation of female leaders.

In our community we found that it wasn't enough to simply say that positions of leadership were open to women. In terms of the teaching ministry we found that while 90% of our small group leaders were women, only 10% of our teachers were women—the reason being that unless a woman had had previous experience in teaching or leadership she generally felt inadequate to the task. What we finally realized was that this fear was not what the Lord wanted, and in fact it was the result of the sinful condition of society which made so many women feel that they were incompetent or intellectually inferior to men. So we had to consciously encourage women to overcome this barrier, to compensate for the effects of this social injustice. And even though half our pastoral team and 40% of our teachers are women, we still feel that we have a way to go in terms of helping women and men to overcome this injustice.

CONCLUSIONS

1. In marriage, the couple discerns what kind of structure they feel God wants for them. There is no divine order of male headship and female submission that applies to all Christians.

2. Women can and should participate in all forms of leadership in the Church (with the exception of the priesthood). This includes all lay associations, prayer groups and charismatic communities.

3. We need to consciously strive to overcome the effects that prejudice and poor teaching have had on the quality of woman's life in the Church. In addition to this we need to create the kind of environment that helps heal the hurts of this social injustice.